Viewfinder
Topics

A United Kingdom?
The Nations of Britain

compiled and edited
by
David Beal

Langenscheidt-Longman
ENGLISH LANGUAGE TEACHING

Viewfinder

Topics

A United Kingdom?

The Nations of Britain

Herausgeber:
Prof. Dr. Peter Freese

Autor:
David Beal, M. A.

Projekt-Team:
David Beal, M. A.
Dr. Peter Dines, Cert. Ed.
Prof. Dr. Hanspeter Dörfel
OStR Dieter Düwel
Prof. Dr. Peter Freese
Dr. Carin Freywald †
Jennifer von der Grün, M. A.
Prof. Dr. Harald Husemann
OStR Reimer Jansen
Michael Mitchell, M. A.
Dr. Michael Porsche
StR Detlef Rediker
StD Dr. Peter-J. Rekowski
OStR i.K. Peter Ringeisen, M. A.
StD Henning Scholz
OStR Dr. Annegret Schrick
OStR Ekkehard Sprenger
OStD Dr. Horst Steur
Donald Turner, M. A.
Philip Wade, M. A., Cert. Ed.

Redaktion:
Dr. Annegret Pago, in Zusammenarbeit mit der Verlagsredaktion Langenscheidt-Longman, Claudia Schwarz, M. A.

Projektleitung Grafik: Beate Andler

Gestaltung und Desktop-Publishing: Barbara Slowik, Atelier S., München

Titelfoto: The national flags of Northern Ireland, Scotland, Wales and England

Umwelthinweis: Gedruckt auf chlorfrei gebleichtem Papier.

1. Auflage 2000

Druck: Mediengruppe Universal GmbH, München
Printed in Germany

ISBN 3-526-50790-2

1 2 3 4 5 / 04 03 02 01 00

Contents

* Titles provided by the editor

Introduction

Behind the apparent unity of the United Kingdom of Great Britain and Northern Ireland lies immense national, cultural, social and historical diversity. It is the aim of this anthology to give some idea of what contributes to this diversity and how it came about.

This subject has become even more topical with the demands for devolution and even independence in Wales and Scotland and the setting up of a Scottish parliament and a Welsh assembly. Northern Ireland, with a devolved parliament from 1921 to 1972, and a population divided on religious, ethnic and political grounds, adds a further dimension.

In dealing with 'the nations of Britain' there is widespread confusion between the terms England, Britain, Great Britain, the United Kingdom and the British Isles. This is partly because geographical entities are mixed up with political ones and partly because England forms the largest part of the UK, both as regards size and population.

In addition, the British state was consolidated by the actions of English kings and rulers, based around London, who first conquered the outlying regions of England from 800-1200 and then Wales and Ireland. They tried but failed to conquer Scotland, which was, however, incorporated by negotiation through the Union of Crowns in 1603, and the Union of Parliaments in 1707.

As a result of all these factors, the country is often referred to as 'England' and its inhabitants as 'the English' – linguistic usage which, if addressed to the Scots and Welsh, might cause a response ranging from amusement to annoyance, or even anger.

This anthology, therefore, emphasises the cultural identities of the Scots, Welsh and Northern Irish and their contribution to the United Kingdom and its history, without neglecting the role of the English. Account is also taken of differing views, often passionately held, about the future of the separate groups within the UK: devolution, federalism, independence, or as in Northern Ireland, union with another state, the Irish Republic.

David Beal

A United Kingdom?

The Nations of Britain

"When people say England, they sometimes mean Great Britain, sometimes the United Kingdom, sometimes the British Isles, – but never England."

George Mikes (1912-1987) Hungarian-born British writer

A Canadian touring Britain in 1989 discovered, in his own words, "There's no such thing as British, only English, Irish, Welsh and Scots."

David McDowell, Britain in Close-up *(Harlow: Longman, 1993), p. 122.*

"It must be remembered that no Englishman, and perhaps no Scot even, calls himself a Briton without a sneaking sense of the ludicrous, or hears himself referred to as a Britisher without squirming. How should an Englishman utter the words Great Britain with the glow of emotion that for him goes with England. His Sovereign may be Her Britannic Majesty to outsiders, but to him is Queen of England."

H.W. Fowler (1858-1933), English lexicographer and grammarian; compiler of Modern English Usage *(1926)*

1 Rudyard Kipling

"The Anvil"

This poem graphically describes the effect the Norman Conquest of 1066 had on England in creating a highly centralised state, and explains why England has, unlike Germany, no tradition of regional autonomy. Rudyard Kipling, *Rudyard Kipling's Verse*: *Definitive Edition* (London: Hodder and Stoughton, 1940), p. 713.

The English are defeated at the Battle of Hastings – 1066. (Bayeux Tapestry)

1 England's on the anvil – hear the hammers ring –
Clanging from the Severn to the Tyne!
Never was a blacksmith like our Norman King –
England's being hammered, hammered, hammered into
line!

England's on the anvil! Heavy are the blows!
(But the work will be a marvel when it's done)
Little bits of Kingdoms cannot stand against their foes.
England's being hammered, hammered, hammered into
one!

There shall be one people – it shall serve one Lord –
(Neither Priest nor Baron shall escape!)
It shall have one speech and law, soul and strength and sword.
England's being hammered, hammered, hammered into
shape!

2 Bernard Crick

"An Englishman's Passport"

In this article Bernard Crick, the respected political scientist and author, discusses the widespread confusion about the name of the country he comes from. – Bernard Crick, *Political Thoughts and Polemics* (Edinburgh: Edinburgh University Press, 1990), pp. 71f.

I am a citizen of a state with no agreed colloquial name. Our passports call us citizens of "The United Kingdom of Great Britain and [Northern] Ireland". But what does one reply when faced by that common existential question of civilised life, which is neither precisely legal nor precisely philosophical, found in foreign hotel registers, "Nationality?"

If that question is meant to establish legal citizenship, then "British" is correct, although that is the least used name colloquially for people as distinct from goods [...] The majority write "English". The overwhelming majority of UK passport holders are, of course, "English", but I have a suspicion that many of them write "English" not as an assertion of nationality, as do those who write "Irish", "Scottish" or "Welsh", but out of a common but mistaken belief that "English" is the adjective corresponding to "citizen of the United Kingdom of Great Britain and Northern Ireland" [...]

Even in documents more elaborate than a passport we English are very confused when we try to name our state. The Central Office of Information publishes an annual handbook on the UK which has all kinds of useful information in it, and has a wide circulation abroad. The title of it is bizarrely (though no one notices or complains) the title of a former Roman province, which has no modern legal or precise geographical meaning: *Britain*. The current Preface of *Britain* states:

Care should be taken when studying British statistics to note whether they refer to England, to England and Wales [...] to Great Britain, which comprises England, Wales and Scotland, or to the United Kingdom (which is the same as Britain, that is Great Britain and Northern Ireland) as a whole.

Indeed. But is "Britain" usually understood to be "the same as" the United Kingdom as a whole? When I say "Britain" I mean, contrary to the C.O.I., the "mainland" only, and say "Great Britain" when I want to include Northern Ireland. Perhaps usage varies. In the *O.E.D.* early usages of Britain all refer to the island or the mainland of the archipelago. And *O.E.D.'s* summary of early modern usage is confused: "The proper name of the whole island, containing England, Wales and Scotland, with their dependencies; more fully called Great Britain; now used for the British state or Empire as a whole." That 'more fully' is as a dictionary entry politically very question-begging and pre-emptive. "Britain" and "Great Britain" are as often used to refer to different entities. Ulster Loyalists are always careful to proclaim their (conditional) loyalty to "Great Britain"or "The United Kingdom"; they rightly suspect that loose talk of "Britain" can often mean the mainland alone, and thus prove a device to distance them, ultimately to separate them.

3 Stanley Baldwin
"England Is the Country and the Country Is England"

This speech was made at the annual dinner of the Royal Society of St. George in 1924, at a time when the power of the British Empire seemed to be at its height, but was already in decline. However, this speech is not so much a celebration of British power but of the English qualities which made this power possible.
Stanley Baldwin, *On England* (London: Philip Allan, 1926), pp. 1-8.

Though I do not think that in the life of a busy man there could be placed into his hands a more difficult toast than this, yet the first thought that comes into my mind as a public man is a feeling of satisfaction and profound thankfulness that I may use the word "England" without some fellow at the back of the room shouting out "Britain". I have often thought how many of the most beautiful passages in the English language would be ruined by that substitution which is so popular today. I read in your Dinner-book, "When God wants a hard thing done, He tells it, not to His Britons, but to His Englishmen". And in the same way, to come to a very modern piece of poetry, how different it would be with the altered ending, "For in spite of all temptations to belong to other nations, he remains a Briton." We have tonight to celebrate our country and our Patron Saint. It always seems to me no mere chance that besides being the Patron Saint of England, St. George was the Patron Saint of those gallant sailors around the shores of the Adriatic, and that in his honour there exists one of the most beautiful chapels in Venice today. The Patron Saint of sailors is surely the most suitable Patron Saint for men of the English stock; and I think tonight amongst ourselves we might for a minute or two look at those characteristics, contradictory often, peculiar as we believe, in that great stock of which we are all members.

The Englishman is all right as long as he is content to be what God made him, an Englishman, but gets into trouble when he tries to be something else. There are chroniclers, or were chroniclers, who said it was the aping of the French manners by our English ancestors that made us the prey of William the Norman, and led to our defeat at Hastings. Let that be a warning to us not to ape any foreign country. Let us be content to trust ourselves and to be ourselves.

[...]

The Englishman is made for a time of crisis, and for a time of emergency. He is serene in difficulties, but may seem indifferent when times are easy. He may not look ahead, he may not heed warnings, he may not prepare, but when he once starts he is persistent to the death, and he is ruthless in action. It is these gifts that have made the Englishman what he is, and that have enabled the Englishman to make England and Empire what it is.

[...]

There is yet one other point. I think the English people are at heart and in practice the kindest people in the world. With some faults on which I have touched, there is in England a profound sympathy for the underdog. There is a brotherly and neighbourly feeling which we see to a remarkable extent through all classes. There is a way of facing misfortunes with a cheerful face. It was shown to a marvellous degree in the war, and in spite of all that he said in criticism of his own people, Ruskin said one thing of immortal truth. He said: "The English laugh is the purest and truest in the metal that can be minted. And indeed only Heaven can know what the country owes to it." There is a profound truth in that. As long as people can laugh, they are preserved from the grosser vices of life, political and moral. As long as they can laugh, they can face all the ills that fortune may bring upon them.

Then, in no nation more than the English is there a diversified individuality. We are a people of individuals, and a people of character. You may take the writings of one of the greatest and one of the most English of writers, Charles Dickens, and you will find that practically all his characters are English. They are all different, and each one of us that has gone through this world with his eyes open and his heart open, has met every one of Dickens's characters in some position or another in life. Let us see to it that we never allow our individuality as Englishmen to be steam-rollered.

4

Peter Hetherington

"Ashington: A Shared Name but Miles Apart"

Ever since the middle of the 19th century the English have been concerned about the north-south divide: the differences and divisions that opened up between the apparently prosperous, largely rural south of England and the north, with its industrial pollution and poverty. This article from *The Guardian*, 6 March 1997 shows that in spite of the many changes that have taken place since then, there are still deep cultural and social divisions between the two parts of the country.

They might be in the same country and share a common name. But in every other respect – from house prices to unemployment – the two Ashingtons, separated by a little over 300 miles, are poles apart.

"We're stuck at opposite ends of the country with little knowledge about life in the other half," says solicitor Brian Norton, who chairs the parish council of Ashington, West Sussex, in the comfortable cradle of the Weald. "We've got this great divide – everything north of Watford is almost foreign – and it seems a bit silly really."

Local councillor and former miner Colin Parker, chairman of the leisure committee in the old northern colliery town of Ashington agrees. "It would be nice to know more about the south, although I would imagine there's a big difference in living standards – we've suffered terribly from pit closures up here."

Yesterday, in a small hall in northern Ashington, they set about bridging that gap with a ten-week course to examine the English divide in microcosm, well-heeled West Sussex (population 2,000) versus down-at-heel Northumberland (population 24,000).

Organised by the Workers' Educational Association, it aims to establish links between the two communities, in the hope of eventually forging twinning-links – and even debunking Disraeli 152 years on: "Two nations, between whom there is no [...] sympathy; who are as ignorant of each other's habits, thoughts and feelings, as if they were dwellers in different zones, or inhabitants of different planets."

The idea came from Bill Gale, an Ashington (Northumberland) community worker who recently stumbled across the West Sussex village of the same name on the A24 between Worthing and Horsham.

He eventually discovered a local historian, Daphne Norton, wife of the parish council chairman, who soon established a liaison group. They began writing to each other and quickly agreed that both communities could gain from sharing experiences.

"While we cannot underestimate this great social divide – there are very stark contrasts – we want to break down taboos," Mr Gale said. "The only thing we seem to have in common, apart from the name, is that we're both close to the sea."

Mrs Norton, who lives in a 14th century farmhouse, finds it hard to visualise the other Ashington, although she thinks she might have passed through it 30 years ago on the way back from Scotland. "I imagine it might be a rather dark and dingy mining town – but no, we think twinning it a rather nice idea, although we thought it was rather hilarious at first."

Ashingtonians who turned up for the launch of yesterday's twinning course were told in a WEA leaflet that they would "explore social, cultural and economic variations ... and reasons and perceptions behind the north-south divide".

Lecturer Ian Rushton said he thought people in the other Ashington were well aware of the fact that they lived in a "relatively well-off commuter belt area".

"It will be interesting to see whether brown ale-swilling

ex-pitmen can be understood south of the Tyne," he joked.

Two teachers, Sheila Little and Gwyn Castiau, were in no doubt that they would. They thought the emerging link with the other Ashington would be an ideal National Curriculum geography project for seven-to-11-year-olds, and they hope to start school exchanges with the Church of England primary school in the Sussex village. "We need to contrast another area of Britain and this seems ideal," said Sheila.

Unlike most other locals, she has lived in the south. "I have to say there is no place like our Ashington. People are much friendlier up here."

Nonsense, retorted David Jenkins, a Tory councillor in Ashington, West Sussex. "You take people as you find them. They're the same all over England, aren't they. Give people the opportunity and they get on, that's what I say – I don't believe in all these handouts." Ashington (Northumberland) winced.

Two nations

	Ashington (Northumberland)	Ashington (West Sussex)
Average semi	£40,000	£85,000
Households with a car	40%	9.9%
Council housing	35%	10.5%
Pubs and clubs	25	2
Famous people	The Charlton brothers	None
Landmark	Woodhorn colliery museum	Hollygate cactus nursery
Local constituency	Wansbeck Labour majority 36%	Horsham Conservative majority 40%
Unemployment	12%	2.8%

The rural South (a typical village)

The industrial North (Newcastle-upon-Tyne)

Info

A British Chronology

700 BC	The Celts arrive in Britain from Europe. The Welsh, Gaelic, Irish and Cornish languages are directly related to the language spoken by the Celts. (See glossary, p. 50)
55,54 BC	Julius Caesar's Roman expedition to Britain. (See glossary, p. 51)
43 AD	Roman conquest of Britain begins under Emperor Claudius.
61	Revolt of Boudicca (or Bodicea) against the Romans.
c406, 410	The Roman army withdraws from Britain.
c450	The Saxons, Angles and Jutes arrive in Britain from what is now Denmark, northern Germany and the Netherlands. (See glossary, p. 51)
470	Celtic monks build the first known monastery in Britain.
470-500	The legendary King Arthur leads the Romano-British or Britons against the Saxons.
450-650	Creation of the Saxon kingdoms of East Anglia, Kent, Sussex, Wessex, Northumbria and Mercia (the present-day Midlands). The Romano-British and Celtic inhabitants flee to Ireland, Wales, Cornwall and Brittany.
597	St Augustine's mission to christianise England arrives in Kent.
787	The Danes (also known as Vikings) begin their attacks on England. Within a hundred years they control most of eastern England. (See glossary, p. 50)
1066	William, Duke of Normandy invades England and defeats the English under Harold at the Battle of Hastings.
1169-72	English conquest of Ireland begins.
1277-84	English conquest of Wales.
1296	The English invade Scotland and Edward I of England declares himself King of Scotland.
1382	The Statute of Pleadings lays down that English (and not Norman French) is to be used in court.
1536-42	Acts of Union integrate England and Wales administratively and legally and give Wales representation in parliament.
1603	Union of the crowns of England and Scotland under James VI of Scotland, who becomes James I of England.
1707	Act of Union unites England and Scotland to form the United Kingdom of Great Britain. The Scottish parliament is abolished.
1801	Act of Union unites Great Britain and Ireland to form the United Kingdom of Great Britain and Ireland.
1921	Ireland is partitioned. The Irish Free State is formed from the 26 southern Irish counties and the six northern counties remain part of Great Britain.
1972	The Northern Ireland parliament at Stormont is suspended and Northern Ireland is governed directly from London.
1997	Referendums in Wales and Scotland support the setting up of a parliament in Scotland and an assembly in Wales.
1998	The Northern Ireland assembly is set up under first minister, David Trimble.
1999	Elections are held for a Scottish parliament and a Welsh assembly. (See "Devolution", p. 22.)

Celtic Cross at Iona Abbey, Scotland

Norman cathedral in Bath

Scene from the film Henry V (Battle of Agincourt, 1415)

5

John C. McIntyre

The Empty Highlands

This poem, which can also be performed as a song, deals with one of the most traumatic events in Scottish history, the periods between 1782 and 1820, and between 1840 and 1854 known as the Highland Clearances. During this time the clan chiefs, who owned most of the Highlands, removed the people who lived and farmed there in order to replace them by the more profitable business of sheep farming. While the chiefs grew rich on selling the meat and wool, the people died of cholera and starvation, or were forced to emigrate abroad.

The Highlands

I have seen the hills of Alba,
a hard and rugged land.
I have seen the stands of Sitka
stretch out on every hand.
I have seen the rocks and mountains,
the lochs and stormy seas.
And I ask myself in wonder:
why is there no-one here?

I have seen the broken fences
in every lonely glen.
I have seen the empty houses
'neath many a glowering ben:
no roofs, no smoke, no chimneys warm,
no children far and near.
And I ask myself in wonder:
Why is there no-one here?

I have seen the golden eagle
And osprey swoop and slay.
I have seen the spitting wildcat
Attack and kill its prey.
I have seen the stags do battle,
Lock horns with little fear.
If scenes like these are Scotland's pride,
Why is there no-one here?

The chiefs of old sold out our rights,
and thus betrayed their kin.
New English lairds bought out the land
and brought new systems in.
They drove away the peasant folk,
For sheep and trees and deer.
So I tell myself in anger:
That's why there's no-one here.

Our oil and fish, our whiskey famed,
are sent to foreign shores.
The profits stay in London town,
and barely let us hope ...
that some day soon, if so we dare,
this land may change, and once again
there may be people here;
that some day soon, if so we dare,
this land may change, and once again
there may be people here.

6 Tom Leonard

" This Is Thi Six A Clock News"

By having a BBC newsreader read the news in the working class dialect of Glasgow, Tom Leonard's poem focuses on the social differences embodied by different dialects. – Tom Leonard, *Selected Work 1965-1983* (London: Vintage, 1984), p. 88.

This is thi
six a clock
news thi
man said n
thi reason
a talk wia
BBC accent
is coz yi
widny wahnt
mi ti talk
aboot thi
trooth wia
voice lik
wanna yoo
scruff. if
a toktaboot
thi trooth
lik wanna yoo
scruff yi
widny thingk
it wuz troo.
jist wanna yoo
scruff tokn.
thirza right
way ti spell
ana right way
to tokit. this
is me tokn yir
right way a
spellin. this
is ma trooth.
yooz doant no
thi trooth
yirselliz cawz
yi canny talk
right. this is
the six a clock
nyooz. belt up.

Working class flats in Glasgow

7 Billy Wolfe

"The Case for Scottish Independence"*

There are three choices open to Scotland in its relationship with England: complete union as has been the case from 1707 until now; transfer or devolution of certain powers to a Scottish parliament, which took place in 2000; and full independence. In this extract Billy Wolfe makes a passionate plea for independence. Billy Wolfe, *Scotland Lives* (Edinburgh: Reprographia, 1973), pp. 166f.

The opportunities before Scotland [...] are all linked together. They depend on the will of the people of Scotland to be a nation again. Not just a provincial part of the "one nation" of the English political parties, but to be a nation again, dynamically, fully, clear of the negation and alienation which have for so long tried to persuade the Scots that to be British is to be internationalist. In fact, it is to be English.

When our children are taught English history instead of Scottish history; when almost every effort of education, from the infant classes to the universities, seems bent on promoting the "one nation" theory and habitual practice of the English Tory and Labour Parties, is it any wonder that people who believe in Scotland feel alienated?

When we see the influence of the daily newspapers and radio programmes as English, in reporting news, in dealing with current affairs, in entertainment of all kinds; when we see Scottish dole queues that are always twice as long as English dole queues; when we see people forced to emigrate, knowing that Scotland's population has risen only 2% in 20 years while England's has risen 11%, Norway's has risen 18% and the USA's has risen 33% in the same period; when we know that in spite of Scotland having had the resources of wealth and the skills, the educational institutions and the brains to have averted the unemployment and that emigration; when we perceive that the decline and stagnation have persisted, all because of the "one nation" theory and practice of the English Parties, is it any wonder that people who believe in Scotland feel alienated?

When we see the deep water facilities of the Clyde ignored; [...] when we see Scotland as a tourist attraction promoted abroad as Angleterre; when we see factory after factory closed down after English take-overs; when we see industry after industry hacked about to fit into an English plan; when we see Budget Day after Budget Day in Westminster prescribing medicine for the English sickness of inflation when Scotland needs the opposite encouragement, having quite different conditions including no balance of payments problem; when we see the possibility of Scotland's great oil wealth not benefiting our country, our people, our nation, and all because of the "one nation" theory and practice of the English Parties, is it any wonder that people who believe in Scotland feel alienated?

In his inaugural address as Rector of Glasgow University, James Reid defined the effects of what he meant by alienation. "It is the cry of men who feel themselves the victims of blind, economic forces beyond their control. It is the frustration of ordinary people excluded from the process of decision-making." I would add alien political and cultural forces to the economic forces, with the proviso that I do not believe that the alien political forces are blind.

Mel Gibson as William Wallace in the film "Braveheart"

An Englishman is a man who lives on an island in the North Sea governed by Scotsmen.

Philip Guedella, The Penguin Book of Modern Humorous Quotations, *comp. Fred Metcalf, (Harmondsworth: Viking 1986), p. 84.*

8 Niall Ferguson

"As a Scot and a Briton, I Fear Today for Our Future"*

Niall Ferguson, a Scot, makes the case for continuing the union between England and Scotland and argues against devolution and independence for Scotland. – *Daily Mail*, 13 September 1997, p. 6.

Yesterday morning [when the results of the referendum on Scottish devolution were announced] I woke up feeling not only a little less Scottish but also a lot less British. I was born in Glasgow of two Scottish parents and four Scottish grandparents and educated at the Glasgow Academy. I look like a Scot, talk like a Scot and am the proud owner of two kilts, one of them inherited from my grandfather who fought in the Great War as a private in the Seaforth Highlanders.

So when Tony Blair and his supporters claim that devolution will strengthen the Union, I know this is unhistorical rubbish. The Union of 1707 was first and foremost a union of parliaments, and any legislation which recreates the Scottish parliament will amount to its repeal.

All that will remain is the union of crowns which occurred in 1603 when James VI of Scotland inherited the English throne from Elizabeth I (herself, please note, from a Welsh family named Tudor).

It was James who came up with the idea of Great Britain. But you don't need a PhD in seventeenth century history to know that the union of crowns by itself was not enough to avert a bloody war between Scotland and England in the 1640s – a conflict which cost James's son Charles I his throne and his head.

Scottish men wearing kilts

Only the union of parliaments could ensure that such a disaster did not recur. One of the crucial reasons for the failure of Charles Edward Stuart's invasion of England in 1745 was that the majority of Lowland Scots did not back him: they had already benefited too much from the peace and prosperity inaugurated by the Act of Union.

We all underestimate at our peril how important that Act has been to our common history as Britons. The English sometimes think "England" and "Britain" are synonymous but that is to understate drastically the contribution Scotland has made over the past 300 years to Britain's extraordinary success story.

It was Scotland's universities which taught the English about free trade and medicine while Oxford and Cambridge slumbered. Without Scottish coal, iron, steel, cotton and ships, England's industrial revolution would have been half-baked.

And never forget that men like my grandfather – Scots in Highland regiments – were always over-represented in the British Army. Without the Jocks, Britain's unparalleled record of military successes would not have been possible. By the same token, Scotland would have been a poorer country if it had remained or returned to being independent: at best a Hungary, at worst a Slovakia and we all know how much better off those two were when linked to their richer, more numerous neighbours, the Austrians and the Czechs.

It was being part of Britain which gave the Scots their opportunities. James Boswell would have been a forgotten Edinburgh lawyer if he had never met Samuel Johnson in London. What would Walter Scott, Thomas Carlyle and John Buchan have been without a wider public to acclaim their genius?

My grandfathers never doubted for a moment that they were at once Scottish and British, and I was raised to feel as loyal to the green and pleasant south as to the craggy, misty north.

I fear that in my lifetime this loyalty may be divided. For if devolution is about strengthening the United Kingdom, why did Alex Salmond, the Scottish National Party leader, give the "Yes Yes" campaign his unqualified support?

The answer is obvious: Mr Salmond (not unreasonably) expects that his party will be the largest opposition party to Labour when the new assembly is elected.

And when the disappointing reality of life under a Labour First Minister dawns on the Scottish voters – it will be the old Strathclyde Regional Council writ large – the SNP will be well placed to argue for full independence.

This week, 60 per cent of the Scottish electorate voted, of which 74 per cent said Yes to devolution.

In other words, just four per cent of the British electorate voted to repeal the Act of Union. (I, by the way, didn't have a vote because although I am Scottish, I did not qualify to have a say as I live in England). Some "people", some "mandate".

What is more, they did not vote for carefully drafted legislation. Yet the devil will lie in the detail – and when the arguments about English tax-payers' huge subsidies to Scotland begin, they will be very hard to stop.

Make no mistake: Mr Dewar is right that Thursday was "one of the most important days in our country's long history".

But the country in question is the United Kingdom of Great Britain and Northern Ireland; and Mr Dewar's bogus appeal to "the Scottish people" may one day prove to have been that country's death sentence.

...the noblest prospect which a Scotchman ever sees is the high road that leads him to England!

Samuel Johnson (1709-1784), English lexicographer, quoted in James Boswell, The Life of Samuel Johnson *(1791) (New York, Toronto: Everyman's Library, 1992), p. 268.*

Info

Famous Scots

Sir William Wallace (c1270-1305), Scottish national hero, the leader of Scottish resistance to King Edward I of England. His army defeated the English at Stirling in 1297. After Edward's second invasion of Scotland in 1298 Wallace was defeated and subsequently executed. His story is told in the film *Braveheart.*

Robert I, also known as Robert the Bruce (1274-1329), reigned 1306-1329. He campaigned against Edward I of England and defeated his son, Edward II at Bannockburn in 1314. He went on to establish Scotland as a separate kingdom.

John Knox (1505-72), a Protestant reformer who played a central part in the establishment of the Church of Scotland within a Scottish Protestant state, and led opposition to the Catholic Mary, Queen of Scots when she returned to Scotland to rule in her own right.

Bonnie Prince Charlie

Charles Edward Stuart (1720-88), also known as Bonnie Prince Charlie or the Young Pretender; he claimed the British throne and led the Jacobite (= in support of James Stuart, his father) uprising of 1745-46. He invaded England with an army largely made up of Catholic Highlanders but was driven back and defeated at the Battle of Culloden, the last important battle on British soil.

Adam Smith (1723-90), economist and philosopher and often regarded as the founder of modern economics. He advocated minimal state interference in economic affairs. Notable works are *Inquiry into the Nature and Causes of the Wealth of Nations* (1776).

James Watt (1736-1819), steam engineer; among his many innovations he greatly improved the efficiency of the steam engine developed by Newcomen, enabling it to be used for a variety of purposes. He introduced the term 'horsepower'. The unit of power the 'watt' is named after him.

Robert Burns (1759-96), poet best known for poems such as *The Jolly Beggars* (1786) and *Tam o' Shanter* (1791) and for old Scottish songs which he collected, including *Auld Lang Syne*. Burns night celebrations are held in Scotland and elsewhere on his birthday 25 January.

Sir Walter Scott (1771-1832), novelist and poet. He established the form of the historical novel in Britain and was influential in his treatment of rural themes and use of regional speech. Notable novels include *Waverley* (1814), *Ivanhoe* (1819), and *Kenilworth* (1821).

Dr David Livingstone (1813-73), missionary and explorer; he went to South Africa in 1841 and then moved northwards. On extensive travels he discovered Lake Ngami, the Zambezi River and the Victoria Falls (named after Queen Victoria). After having got lost in his search for the source of the Nile he was found by the American journalist, Sir Henry Morton Stanley in 1871 and supposedly greeted with the words: "Dr Livingstone, I presume."

Robert Louis Stevenson

Robert Louis Stevenson (1850-94), poet, novelist and travel writer; he made his name with the adventure story *Treasure Island* (1883). Other notable works are *The Strange Case of Dr Jekyll and Mr Hyde*, and *Kidnapped* (both 1886).

Sean Connery (1937-), after serving in the Royal Navy he became a film actor and appeared in nine films from 1956 to 1963. He is best known for his portrayal of James Bond in *Dr No* (1963), *From Russia with Love* (1964), *Goldfinger* (1965), *Thunderball* (1965), *You Only Live Twice* (1967), *Diamonds are Forever* (1971) and *Never Say Never Again* (1981). He has recently been an active supporter of the Scottish National Party.

Hadrian's Wall

Info

A Scottish Chronology

10th C. B.C.	Scotland is settled by Celtic tribes, including the Picts.
81 AD	The Romans under General Agricola advance into Scotland as far as the Forth-Clyde line.
ca. 120 AD	Hadrian builds the wall which bears his name to protect the Roman provinces of Britain from Celtic tribes in what is now Scotland.
ca. 250	Scotland is invaded by the Scotti, a Celtic tribe from Ireland who gave the country its name.
ca. 350	The Picts and the Scots break through Hadrian's Wall into England.

300-600	The Picts and Scots are converted to Christianity.
832-60	The Scots and Picts merge under Kenneth MacAlpine to form what is to become the kingdom of Scotia.
1005	Malcolm II becomes king of the Picts and the Scots.
1040	Duncan, the grandson of Malcolm, is murdered by Macbeth.
1296	Edward I of England invades Scotland. The Stone of Scone, or Stone of Destiny, on which Scottish kings had been invested with royal authority, is taken to England and placed in Westminster Abbey.
1297	The Scots under William Wallace defeat the English at Stirling Bridge but fail to stop their advance.
1314	The Scots under Robert the Bruce defeat the English at the Battle of Bannockburn; Scotland becomes completely independent.
1320	The Declaration of Arbroath affirms Scottish independence.
1320	Robert the Bruce calls the first Scottish parliament, consisting of clergy, barons and representatives of the towns.
1560	Founding of the Presbyterian (Protestant) Church in Scotland.
1603	Elizabeth I of England dies childless. James VI of Scotland becomes James I of England. The Union of Crowns.
1688	James II is overthrown and flees to France. William and Mary of Orange are invited to become King and Queen of England.
1707	The Act of Union unites the Scottish and English parliaments. No changes are made to the Scottish religious system and Scotland retains its separate legal tradition. England, Scotland and Wales become the United Kingdom of Great Britain.
1715	First Jacobite rebellion in support of James Edward Stuart.
1745	Second Jacobite rebellion in support of Charles Edward Stuart (Bonnie Prince Charlie). He tries, with the help of the Scottish Highlanders, to win back the crown of Britain for the Stuarts by leading an uprising in Scotland and an invasion of England. He is finally defeated at the Battle of Culloden, near Inverness.
ca.1750-1850	Emigration from Scotland. Highland Clearances 1782 - 1820 and 1840 - 1854. The people of the Highlands are forced to emigrate to make room for sheep farms. Highlanders emigrate to England and North America.
ca.1830-1890	Emigration from Scotland to Australia, New Zealand, Canada, South Africa, and the USA.
1885	The Scottish Office, under the Secretary of State for Scotland, is established with responsibility for education, police, prisons, roads, and public health.
1934	Founding of the Scottish National Party (SNP).
1969	The SNP wins its first seat in the British parliament. Oil reserves are found in the North Sea.
1975	The first oil is extracted from the North Sea.
1979	A referendum is held in Scotland on whether Scotland should have its own assembly. As only 32% of the electorate vote for the assembly, and not the 40% required by the government, the proposal is defeated.
1992	The SNP manages to gain 21% of the Scottish vote but only 3 of the 72 Scottish parliamentary seats.
1997	In the referendum on devolution (see info "Devolution", p. 22) Scotland votes by a large majority for a Scottish parliament.
1999	The Scottish parliament is elected and meets in Edinburgh.

9 Michael Williams

"Keeping up with the Joneses"

In this extract Michael Williams deals with Welsh history, the complex nature of Welsh identity, and the relationship of the Welsh with their neighbours, the English. – *BBC Worldwide*, August 1993, pp. 18f.

The name itself, "Welsh", is somewhat dubious. When in the 6th century, pagan Saxon lager-louts jumped ashore from their longships in Kent, they labelled the peaceful, urbanised, Christian Britons (my ancestors) whom they found here "Velschen": Old German for "foreigner", a derogatory word which has the sense of "illegal immigrant". We called ourselves "Cymru": companions.

[...]

These Britons, softened by too many Roman hot baths and unused to fighting after half a millenium of peace, were no match for the land-hungry Teutons. Gradually, with a bit of ethnic cleansing, the Celts were driven west – into what is now Wales, Cornwall and Cumbria. The Welsh, they say, are the Irish who couldn't swim.

Some, wishing to put water between themselves and the Saxons, went to Brittany. The Breton language is closely related to Welsh.

Ever since we have had to live side by side with this extraordinary people, the English. The fact has defined and shaped our attitudes.

We joined these bewildering buccaneers in their global quest for trade and empire. We acknowledged their predominance but kept our sense of difference. Or at least the ordinary folk did. The elite of Wales, the *crachach*, became more English than the English. The magnificent family we today know as the Cecils were Seisyllts when they first drove a flock of sheep to London some time around 1420.

A certain Morgan Williams crossed the border, made friends with the Chancellor Thomas Cromwell and changed his name to that of his patron. His great-grandchild was Oliver Cromwell, regicide and one of the most dynamic figures in British history.

Today, the rifts of history have healed. The Welsh and the English are united (except at football matches) in harmony.

[...]

The understanding has taken time, however. Evelyn Waugh wrote in *Decline and Fall*: "We can trace nearly all the disasters of English history to the influence of the Welsh" – which is somewhat harsh.

The Welsh are Celts, the English Teutons. The two races lie on either side of the great genetic divide in Western Europe. Our cousins are the Irish, the Bretons, the Highland (but not the Lowland) Scots: the English belong to the same blood-stock as the Germans and Scandinavians. In the simplistic schema the Saxon is stolid, open, practical, unimaginative, realistic; the Celt romantic, dreamy, visionary, excitable, wordy.

No one exemplified this division more than David Lloyd George, Prime Minister of Britain from 1916 to 1922. Angel-tongued in both languages he was regarded by the English as a Merlin-like creature from the misty west whose charm was dangerous; a highly sexed creature whom the London establishment saw as "half-man, half-goat" but who was a great war leader. They discarded him as soon as his usefulness was over. Lloyd George was "dynamic" and "dynamism can be a very destructive force", as the man who displaced him – the very Saxon Stanley Baldwin – charged.

The popular phrase was "Lloyd George knew my father" and it is not too difficult to believe, for Wales is compact indeed. It is possible to drive from the northern tip to the southern-most shore between breakfast and lunch.

Everyone knows everyone, or at least one has met their second cousin twice removed. We have a severe shortage of surnames. This goes back to the middle ages. Welshmen called themselves after their father's and grandfather's first names, so when the English bailiff demanded that of the tenant for his register, out would come "Lewis ap [son of] Howell ap Gruffydd ap ..."

"Good God, man," some tax gatherer must have snorted one day in about 1325, "you must have a proper handle. I'll tell you what, you take the name of your overlord as your surname." The barons of the day being called William, John, David, Edward, we ended up being registered as Williams, Jones, Davies, Edwards and so on. So a Welsh reunion often becomes a form of verbal blind man's buff. "Oh, you mean the John Roberts who married Bronwen Jones, not the John Roberts who went to New Zealand ..."

That is why we tend to stick functional nicknames on to people: Watkins Meat (for the butcher) or Lloyd Lookout (coastguard). A baker who went to Buckingham Palace to receive his MBE from the Queen was known thereafter as Rhys Upper Crust. One Caernarfon pensioner who had a single prominent tooth in the middle of his gum was christened Dai Central Eating. Lynn Davies, Britain's holder of the record for the long jump, is known universally as "Lynn the Leap".

In Welsh life, sociability binds groups together. There is little class distinction. That is not to say that people do not think that they are "better" than other people but there is a lack of the glass walls that can suddenly appear in the drawing-rooms in Anglian suburbia.

Much is made, for instance, of academic achievement. Springing from a land which produced sheep, thin black cattle and little else, human brains had to be exploited.

Every cottage, it was said, housed a clergyman, a teacher or a pig. The drive was to study hard, pass the exams and get a job, preferably from the state or local authority. Learning, however, was and is valued for its own sake.

It is not an uncommon thing to find the postman an expert on medieval poetry or the undertaker able to reel off the names of the Princes of Powys back to the Flood.

At the annual tribal gathering, the National Eisteddfod, the bardic chair is competed for and won by people engaged in the ordinary work of the community. The culture is literary and somewhat backward-looking but it is deep and widespread. Unfortunately, like all civilised life, it is threatened by Coca-Cola culture and MTV.

Tiny as it is, Wales is two distinct nations. In the north, we tend to be introverted, dreamy, religious, "addicted to cheese on toast and guilt" but keen-witted interested (obsessed, perhaps) by the written and spoken word, tight with money, suspicious and abstemious. In contrast the South Walian is extrovert, sociable, deep-drinking, carefree. They are mostly factory workers, whereas we northerners tend to be peasants. Up here, the chapel was the mainstay of the community; down south it was the Social Club and the Miners' Institute.

But rugby unites us. We all rejoiced during the golden days when Welsh teams bestrode the world. We share the pain of recent days.

After the national humiliation of defeat by Western Samoa ("What would the score have been if it was the whole of Samoa?" wits jeered), my uncle Huw retired to bed for a fortnight with a black crepe band on the arm of his winceyette pyjamas. His wife brought him only food that could be eaten with a wooden spoon, as she feared he might do dreadful things to himself if he had access to a knife and a fork.

The land itself inspires a common loyalty: bounded by the sea on three sides, Wales shares a land border with England on the fourth. There are, indeed, hideous scars where the industrial revolution scorched the valleys. Artificial hills of coal and slate waste mark the places where the earth was raped with a brutality shocking to our environmentally conscious generation.

Away from these places of desolation there are magnificent hills, valleys of a quiet, emerald green softness, lakes from whose waters you would not be surprised to see an arm emerge, clad in white samite, to catch Excalibur; silvery beaches where mermaids might sit and blow-dry their golden split-ends.

"Why, Lord, did you make Cwm Pennant so beautiful and the life of an old shepherd so short?" complained one of our bards. There are places that make the heart stop still.

[...]

David Lloyd George

10

Jan Morris

"The Welsh Dragon"*

Most nations have a symbol which tells us something about its character and its history. In this extract from her book *The Matter of Wales*, the Welsh travel writer and historian, Jan Morris tells us about the origins and meaning of the symbol of Wales, the dragon. – Jan Morris, *The Matter of Wales* (Harmondsworth: Penguin, 1986), pp. 28-30.

There is no questioning the identity of the Red Dragon, the ultimate chimera, for he is the national creature of Wales. Not only does he bestride the national flag of green and white, but he supports innumerable coats of arms, embellishes a host of logos, ennobles beer bottles, dominates posters, is sold to tourists in a thousand guises, ash-trays to door-knockers, and has been emblazoned on the uniforms of Welsh soldiers for hundreds of years. Dragons twisted in ironwork, rampant on gateposts, give many a civic building in Wales its authoritative air; a musical apotheosis of the dragon is afforded by the organ at Usk Church, for every one of its pipes is moulded into a dragon's head, from the mighty monsters of the great diapasons to the squeaky infant creatures of the treble. Comical Welshmen dress up as the Red Dragon sometimes, and prance on to rugby football pitches, and the dragon welcomes every visitor to Wales on the road signs along the border - Croeso i Gymru! it says, sticking out its forked tongue and raising an admonitary claw - "Welcome to Wales!"

There have always been dragons in this country. Dragons, we learn from the medieval mnemonics called the Triads, were among the Three Things One Does Well to Hide, and the last live one was reported to have spent his nights in the church tower of Llandeilo Graban in Powys, which does have a dragon-chamber near the top of it. Sometimes the dragons of Wales have been vile, sometimes very beautiful. The dragon called the carrog which gave its name to the village of Dol-y-Garrog in Gwynedd was so malicious that when at last it was hunted down and killed, even in death one of its teeth fatally poisoned a man who kicked its carcass. On the other hand the winged serpents of Llancarfan in Glamorgan, though they were as pestilential as foxes, were said to have crests that shone with all the colours of the rainbow, and wings like feathers of a peacock's tail, and when they were disturbed they "glided swiftly, sparkling all over, to their hiding places".

This is how the Red Dragon became the national beast of Wales. In the heart of Eryri in Gwynedd, a few miles north of Beddgelert, a hillock beside the road marks the traditional site of Dinas Emrys, an ancient seat of Welsh power. Here the king Gwyrtheyrn, Vortigern, laid the foundations of a new capital, but hardly had his builders started work on it than all its stones disappeared. Repeatedly, they tried, repeatedly their materials vanished, until the young Myrddin, Merlin the magician, disclosed the reason why. Dig beneath the ground, he said, and they would find a pool, and in the pool there would be a tent, and in the tent two sleeping dragons, one white, one red. They did as they were told, and there were the two dragons, and they awoke, and they fought each other, writhing in the tent and in the pool, until they disappeared from the hill. "The white dragon is the Saxon," pronounced Merlin, "the red dragon is Cymru, and so they will fight, the red against the white, until at last the dragon of Wales is triumphant over the dragon of the Saxons." The king, he said, must build his city somewhere else: and so it was that while Dinas Emrys is only a wooded tump, with a public footpath up its flank, the Red Dragon lives on as Myrddin prophesied, still the champion of the Welsh, and still squabbling with its ancient enemy.

But others say that the Welsh Dragon is descended directly from the purple griffin of the Roman imperial banners, and that the Welsh national flag is therefore the oldest on earth.

"The Welsh Dragon" (at the Rugby World Championships)

1

R. Gerallt Jones

"The Letter"

Wales is a bilingual country. Everybody speaks English and there are about 500,000 people who speak Welsh; for most of them it is their first language. This extract from a short story, originally written in Welsh and translated into English by the author, tells of a Welsh-speaking boy's first confrontation with an English school and English-speaking schoolboys. – R. Gerallt Jones, "The Letter", in *Classic Welsh Stories*, eds. Gwyn Jones and Islwyn Ffowc Elis (Oxford: Oxford University Press, 1992), pp. 57-61.

[...] now I was going as well. No more walking between the hedges to school. What did 'away' mean? Was it farther than Pwllheli? Perhaps it was as far as Bangor. Math said that the name of the place was Shwsbri, but that meant nothing. It sounded a bit like strawberries, and strawberries could be found in Llaniestyn, if only in Mr Barret's garden. Would it be possible to fish in the pond after being 'away', or to sit on the bridge, or to go to Felin Eithin shop to buy fresh bread and eat all the crust on the way home? Could I play trains in the front room? Clic-di-clac, clic-de-clac. Oh, Mam, I don't want to go to Shwsbri. "Dear Mam. I don't know where I'll be when you receive this letter. I have jumped off the train. I am going to India because I don't want to go to Shwsbri away to school. Yours truly ..."

I fling down the *Hotspur*, stare indignantly at Criccieth station outside, and attack my meat sandwich. It must be hours and hours since I had breakfast.

At Dovey Junction, when I have more or less forgotten the end-product of the journey, and am poking around the platform happily enough, what do I see in the middle of a crowd of people but a school cap. Exactly the same colour as the sparkling new cap which is safely tucked away in my own pocket. I stand stock still. Then I creep back step by step round the corner of the gents. I stand there for a minute, my heart pumping away and my breath catching in my throat. Another boy going to the same place! Who is he? He looks incredibly clever and beautiful in his cap. I peer around the corner of the gents to look at him. He is standing in the middle of the platform, with a new, leather case by his side. And what is he doing? Reading a newspaper! The only one I have ever seen reading a newspaper is my father. And my father is old. Do boys read newspapers in Shwsbri? Dear God, what sort of place am I going to?

When the Shwsbri train comes in, I jump smartly into an empty compartment near the back. Please God, I say, don't send that boy into this compartment. But I know perfectly well that it is no good. He arrives soon enough, swaggering his way down the corridor, cap over one ear. And in he comes. After flinging his bag up in the rack overhead and settling himself in a corner, he gives me the once-over, like a farmer at the stock-market.

"I see we're going to the same place," he says off-handedly, pointing at the corner of my new cap that's peeping stupidly out of my coat pocket. "I goin' to Shwsbri," I volunteer.

"Yes, old son, we're all going there on this train," he says, "but you and I are going to the same school."

"Oh. Yes." There are too many English words chasing each other across his lips for me to follow properly. I can do nothing but sit and stare stupidly at his middle. Oh, Mam, I don't want to go away to old school, where they talk funny and boys with newspapers and no damn anybody speaking Welsh. Diawl, diawl, diawl, I say, leaning heavily on my lonely obscenity. I don't want to go to old school.

"I s'pose you're a new boy," he offers, after a dreadful, long pause.

"Yes."

"Mm. Well, you ought to be wearing your cap, you know. It's an offence not to wear your cap."

"Oh." I grab my black and yellow cap and stick it on my head.

"Offence?"

"Offence. Crime. Breaking the rules. What's the matter, don't you understand English?"

But the question does not require an answer, and he snuggles up behind his papers and comics to chew sweets and whistle tunelessly from time to time to show that he remembers I'm here. In Welshpool, three others descend on us, everyone laughing madly, thumping backs, pumping hands, and speaking a totally incomprehensible language, with words like 'swishing' and 'brekker' and 'footer' and 'prep'. After they've had their fill of taking each other's caps and kicking each other and flinging cases back and forth, someone notices me.

"What's this, Podge, freshie?"

"Yes," says the veteran. "Welshie as well. Can't understand a word of English."

"Good God." He gets up and stands in front of me and

But Lord! to see the absurd nature of Englishmen, that cannot forbear laughing and jeering at everything that looks strange.

Samuel Pepys (1633-1703), diarist, "Diary 27 November 1662" in The Bloomsbury Chronological Dictionary of Quotations, *ed. Edmund Wrights, (London: Bloomsbury, 1993), p. 126.*

stares into my face. I can see the blackspots in the end of his nose. By this time everyone is listening intently. He holds his face within three inches of mine. If I was brave, I would knock his teeth down his throat. If I was like Math or the Saint. But I'm not.

"Welshie are you? Welsh? Welsh?"

"Yes," I say sadly, "I am from Pen Llyn."

Everyone starts hooting with laughter, rolling around on their seats. The questioner tries again.

"Going to Priestley School are you? School? School?"

"Yes."

He turns triumphantly to the others.

"Bloody hell, fellers, we'll have some fun with this when we get there. All it can say is yes."

And everyone starts rolling with laughter once again. I push myself far back into my corner for the remainder of the journey, feel the damn silly wetness in my eyes, and try to think about Cannonball Kidd, about caravans, about Barmouth, about anything but Mam and Pen Llyn this morning. Clic-di-clac, clic-di-clac. "Remember to write a letter." Clic-di-clac, remember to write.

When the train reaches Shwsbri station, they all forget about me soon enough, and the whole gang rushes out on the platform, their bags flying in all directions, caps shining new in the rain, everyone talking. On the platform, standing stiff as a poker, there's an ugly woman in a feathered hat, her lips one grim line, and a thin black walking stick in her hand. As each one of them sees her, he stops dead, pulls his cap straight, hauls trousers up, tries to get everything back into line.

"Well." She looks at them as though she suddenly smells something unpleasant. "Isn't there anyone else with you?"

Then she sees me standing in the carriage door, cap in hand, and my tie round the back of my neck.

"Oh." With a come-and-gone smile flashing across her white teeth. "Here he is. Are you Jones?"

"Yes, missus. My name is Joni Jones."

"I see. Well, from now on you'll be Jones. Jones J. We don't use names like Johnnie at school, do we? And nice little boys don't say missus, Jones. My name is Miss Darby. Now boys, let's be on our way. We'll all be ready for tea, I have no doubt."

And off she goes along the platform, her stick clicking up and down, and her bottom waddling regularly from side to side like a duck's. And everyone follows her quiet as mice, and me following everyone else like Mrs Jones the Post's little terrier dog.

Snowdonia, North Wales

I don't remember much about the next two days, thank God, only an occasional minute here and there. But I know very well that it's all far worse than any nightmare I've ever had about the place before I got here. And I had plenty of those. Everyone in this Priestley looks old and very experienced and talks a mouthful of English. The teachers have never heard of Wales, I don't think, and the cabbage is tough as string and black and green like water-cress, and the bed is hard as sleeping on the floor, and the headmaster teaches something called Latin in a room with iron bars across the windows. Every night before going to bed I go to the lavatory to cry quietly and then go back to that cold barn where everyone is pretending to sleep, and waiting to bait the Welshie.

On Sunday, we are all gathered together in the Latin room with a piece of paper and a small square envelope each, and the head tells us to write a letter home to say we are all right, have arrived safe and have had enough to eat. Well, I grab my brand new fountain-pen, and start

Dear Mum and Dad,

I hope you are o.k. like me. I have arrived safe. The food is quite good and the school is quite nice. I am looking forward to the holidays. Remember me to Spot and to Llyn y Felin.

This in brief,
Joni.

Info

Famous Welsh people

Owain Glyn Dwr (English: Owen Glendower) (c1354-c1417), a Welsh chief who proclaimed himself Prince of Wales and led a national uprising against Henry VI of England.

David Lloyd George (1863-1945), prime minister of Great Britain 1916-22 and chancellor of the exchequer 1908-15. As chancellor he introduced old-age pensions in 1908 and national insurance for health and unemployment in 1911.

Aneurin "Nye" Bevan (1897-1960), was born in Tredegar, South Wales and began working as a miner at the age of 13. He was Labour MP for Ebbw Vale in the South Wales and a key figure in the 1945-51 Labour government. As minister of health he created the National Health Service (1948).

Dylan Thomas (1914-53), his most famous work is *Under Milk Wood*, a portrait of a small Welsh town, interspersing alliterative prose with songs and ballads, which he first narrated on radio in 1953. Other notable works are *Portrait of the Artist as a Young Dog* (1940) and a number of poems.

Richard Burton (1925-84), actor; born Richard Jenkins. He often co-starred with Elizabeth Taylor (to whom he was married twice). Notable films were: *The Spy Who Came in from the Cold* (1966) and *Who's Afraid of Virginia Woolf* (1966).

Info

A Welsh Chronology

c700 BC The first Celts arrive in Britain (see glossary p. 50).

c770 Offa, the king of the Saxon kingdom of Mercia, constructs the wall known as Offa's Dyke, to form a barrier between the Saxons and the Welsh. It runs the whole length of the border between England and Wales for over a hundred and twenty miles.

1282 The end of the second Welsh war of Edward I of England; the death of the Welsh leader, Prince Llewelyn, and defeat of the Welsh armies.

1301 After defeating the native princes of Wales, King Edward I of England names his son Prince of Wales. Since then the eldest son of the king or queen of England has traditionally been given this title.

1400-10 The revolt of Owain Glyn Dwr.

1404 Glyn Dwr calls an all-Welsh parliament together.

1536 Wales is brought into the English system of national and local government by an Act of Union. The Bible is translated into Welsh.

1850s The industrial revolution completely changes the face of South Wales. Workers come in from England and Ireland. The main industries are coal mining, iron and steel making and tinplate manufacture.

1872 The first college of what was to become the University of Wales is established in Aberystwyth.

1921 The University of Wales has colleges at Bangor, Aberystwyth, Cardiff and Swansea.

1925 Founding of Plaid Cymru, the Welsh nationalist party.

1970s Beginning of the decline of the traditional heavy industries of South Wales: coal, steel, engineering and textiles.

1973 The Welsh language is given equality with English for all purposes by the Welsh Language Act.

1982 A television station broadcasting in Welsh is established.

1997 The Welsh vote by a small majority to set up a Welsh assembly.

1999 The Welsh elect an assembly, which meets in Cardiff.

Coal mine in South Wales

12 Stephen Castle
"After Devolution, Not Revolution But Evolution"

This newspaper article discusses some of the ways in which the creation of a Scottish parliament and a Welsh assembly may affect the way England is governed. In the meantime, on 12 May 1999, both of these bodies were elected and are now functioning. *The Independent on Sunday*, 14 September 1997, p. 17.

Encouraged by their success in Scotland last week, the government plans further local reforms, starting in London. A powerful London mayor would quickly emerge as a significant national figure.

After the result came the hyperbole. In the aftermath of the stunning success of Scotland's devolutionists, politicians of all descriptions lost little time predicting a new dawn for British politics.

The vote, according to the Welsh Office minister Peter Hain, spelled the end of the "anachronistic rituals and centralising elitism of the old system". His backbench colleague, Fraser Kemp, predicted a new urgency "to get moving on a directly elected assembly for the north of England". And the Conservative former Cabinet minister, John MacGregor, warned that the move would "inevitably" lead to an English Parliament.

But will changes in Scotland and (assuming this week's referendum goes as expected) in Wales really have a profound effect on England? The answer appears to be yes, although the precise shape of British politics in 10 or 20 years' time is impossible to predict. Even among Labour's architects of constitutional change the implications of recent events have barely been thought through.

For decades the Labour Party has tied itself up in knots over devolution. Central to its difficulties has been the relationship between England and Scotland. It was in the 1970s that Tam Dalyell, the veteran anti-devolutionist, coined his famous West Lothian question. The difficulty, he pinpointed, was the relationship between Scotland's new Parliament, and its continuing representation at Westminster: Why, Dalyell asked, should an MP representing a Scottish constituency be able to vote on education in England, but have no voice over policy at the schools in his constituency? (Under devolution, those responsibilities will, of course, be devolved to a Scottish Parliament with a separate membership.)

In the 1992 general election manifesto, Labour's answer to the West Lothian conundrum was that England, as well as Wales, would have elected regional assemblies too. After the election defeat that pledge was speedily dropped. There was little evidence of demand for regional voices. Instead, Labour policy-makers concentrated on efforts to democratise the bureaucracy which administered central government initiatives and quangos in 10 English regions – the so-called regional government offices. Even that has now been scaled back, leaving the West Lothian issue as live as ever.

In the short term this has two important implications. The first is that the number of MPs Scotland can send to Westminster will be reviewed by the next Boundary Commission, and almost certainly reduced.

The second concerns the formula under which Scotland received more generous funding from the Treasury than English regions, in deference to its geographical size. In the next couple of years there will be no change, but the government has given no commitment to retain this arrangement. "No departmental spending can be exempt from review," said one government source last week. That means funding for Scotland is almost certain to come under attack.

England, however, will have new structures in the regions.The most important of these – the only one which will be directly elected – will be in London, where the government wants to create a new, relatively small assembly for the capital, and a New York-style city mayor. Government plans to legislate for these changes will be put to the test in a London referendum next year on local election day, 7 May. If, as expected, the plans go ahead, a powerful London city mayor, with an inevitably high media profile, would quickly emerge as a significant national figure. That, almost inevitably, would prompt other cities to copy the London experiment.

Then there are the economic initiatives being planned by the deputy prime minister, John Prescott. His priority is to create a network of nine regional development agencies. Details of the duties and powers of these bodies, which will dispose of the £5.6bn currently spent on development in the regions, have yet to be decided.

By switching the focus to economic regeneration Mr. Prescott is hoping for evolutionary, rather than revolutionary, change. His allies point out that his reform will bring the English regions into line with Scotland and Wales, which have both had successful development agencies since the 1970s. Repeating their success, says one minister, is the vital pre-requisite of "closing the democratic deficit".

Here the government is treading carefully. Where it once wanted full democratisation of government regional offices, now it proposes regional chambers to work in tandem with them. These will be made up of business, trade union and local authority representatives.

[...]

Yet perhaps the most important aspect of the constitutional changes now under way lies in the changed voting systems they will produce. In London the election of a city mayor may force the political parties to adopt US-style primaries to select their official candidate. Both the Scottish and Welsh bodies are destined to have a more proportional system of electing their new members.

[...]

Meanwhile, government moves to reform the voting system for the European elections, and the possibility of PR for local elections in Scotland, will also make the first-past-the-post system at Westminster look increasingly anomalous.

[...]

"Change," said one Minister last week, "may not come next year or the year after, but it will be unstoppable". That, of course, assumes that devolution retains much of the support it won last Thursday in Scotland.

One country, three systems

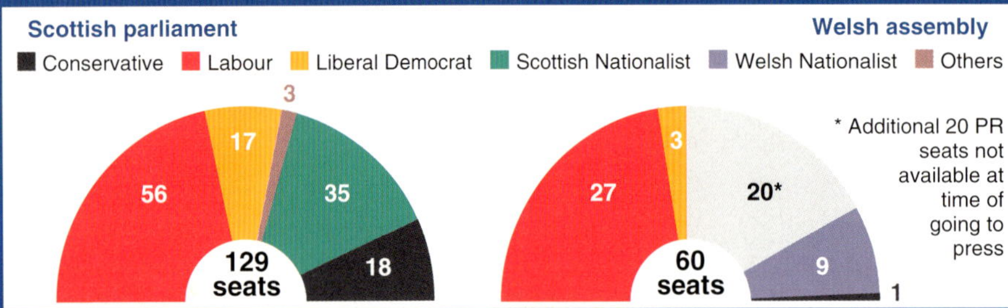

The Scottish parliament

- Has 129 members meeting in Edinburgh
- Elections every four years
- 73 members elected from parliamentary constituencies
- A top-up of 56 from eight electoral regions, seven from each
- Budget of £14bn-£15bn

It has control over

- Criminal and civil law
- Police
- Health
- Education
- Training policy
- Housing
- Planning
- Economic developement
- Financial assistance to industry
- Tourism
- Some aspects of transport
- Environment
- National heritage
- Agriculture, forestry and fisheries
- Arts

The Welsh assembly

- Has 60 members meeting in Cardiff
- Elections every four years
- 40 members elected from parliamentary constituencies
- A top-up of 20 from five electoral regions, four from each
- Budget of about £7bn, similar to current Welsh Office

It has control over

- Health
- Education
- Training policy
- Housing
- Planning
- Economic developement
- Financial assistance to industry
- Tourism
- Some aspects of transport
- Environment
- National heritage
- Agriculture, forestry and fisheries
- Arts

The Westminster parliament

- House of Commons has 659 MPs meeting in London
- Elections at least every five years
- All elected by non-proportional system
- Budget of about £328bn

It has control over

- Foreign policy
- Defence and national security
- Stability of [...], economic and monetary system
- Border control
- Drug policy
- Common markets for UK goods and services
- Electricity, coal, oil, gas and nuclear energy
- Transport safety and regulations
- Social security policy and administration
- Employment legislation
- Abortion
- Broadcasting
- Equal opportunities

Info

Devolution – The 1997 Referendum Results

Scotland

Question 1:

I agree that there should be a Scottish parliament

Yes	1,775,045	74.3 %
No	614,400	25.7 %

Question 2:

I agree that a Scottish parliament should have tax varying powers

Yes	1,512,889	63.5 %
No	870,263	36.5 %

Turnout:

Question 1	60.2 %
Question 2	60.0 %

Wales

I agree that there should be a Welsh assembly

Yes	559,419	50.3 %
No	552,698	49.7 %

Turnout: 51.3 %

13 "The Ould Orange Flute"

While the conflict between the Protestant and Catholic communities in Northern Ireland is usually portrayed as harsh and violent, it does have its lighter side. This traditional ballad from Northern Ireland tells the humorous story of a young Protestant who married a Catholic girl. Although usually sung by Catholics, and therefore considered to be an ironic comment on Protestant bigotry, it could also be taken as a compliment to Protestant endurance. – Joe McPartland (ed.), *The Ulster Reciter* (Belfast: The Blackstaff Press, 1984), pp. 57f.

In the County Tyrone, near the town of Dungannon,
Where many's the ruction myself had a han' in,
Bob Williamson lived, a weaver by trade,
And all of us thought him a stout Orange blade.
On the Twelfth of July, as it yearly did come,
Bob played on the flute to the sound of the drum.
You may talk of your harp, your piano or lute,
But nothing could sound like the ould orange flute.

But Bob the deceyver, he took us all in,
For he married a Papish called Bridget McGinn,
Turned Papish himself, and forsook the ould cause
That gave us our freedom, religion and laws.
Now, the boys in the townland made comment upon it,
And Bob had to fly to the province of Connaught.
He flew with his wife, and his fixin's to boot,
And along with the others the ould Orange flute.

At the Chapel on Sundays to atone for past deeds,
He said "Paters" and "Aves" and counted his beads,
Till, after some time, at the priest's own desire,
He went with his ould flute to play in the choir,
He went with his ould flute to play in the Mass,
But the instrument shivered and sighed, Oh alas!
When he blew it and fingered and made a great noise,
The flute would play only "The Protestant Boys".

Bob jumped and he started and got in a splutter,
And he threw the ould flute in the Bless'd Holy Water;
He thought that this charm might bring some other sound.
When he blew it again, it played "Croppies lie down",
And all he could whistle and finger and blow,
To play Papish music he found it no go.
"Kick the Pope", "The Boyne Water" and such like it would sound,
But one Papish squeak in it couldn't be found.

At a council of priests that was held the next day,
They decided to banish the ould flute away;
For they couldn't knock heresy out of its head,
And they bought Bob another to play in its stead.
So the ould flute was doomed and its fate was pathetic;
It was fastened and burned at the stake as a heretic.
While the flames roared around it, they heard a strange noise –
'Twas the ould flute still whistlin' "The Protestant Boys"!

A parade of Protestant Orangemen

An Englishman arrives in Northern Ireland and is immediately asked: "Are you a Protestant or a Catholic?"
"Well, actually, I'm Jewish."
"Yes, but are you a Protestant Jew or a Catholic Jew?

Traditional saying

14 Bernard MacLaverty
"Walking the Dog"

The conflict between the Protestant and Catholic communities in Northern Ireland, which reached new heights during the Troubles of 1969-1998, involved violence and murder by both sides. This extract vividly illustrates the atmosphere of violence in the province. – Bernard MacLaverty, *Walking the Dog* (Harmondsworth: Penguin, 1995), pp. 4-10.

"Get in," the guy said.

"What?"

"Get in the fuckin car." He was beckoning with one hand and the other was pointing. Not pointing but aiming a gun at him. Was this a joke? Maybe a starting pistol.

"Move or I'll blow your fuckin head off." The dog saw the open door and leapt into the back seat of the car. A voice shouted from inside,

"Get that hound outa here."

"Come on. Get in," said the guy with the gun. "Nice and slow or I'll blow your fuckin head off."

Car headlights were coming in the opposite direction. The driver shouted to hurry up. The guy with the gun grabbed him by the back of the neck and pushed – pushed his head down and shoved him into the car. And he was in the back seat beside his dog with the gunman crowding in beside him.

"Get your head down." He felt a hand at the back of his neck forcing his head down to his knees. The headlights of the approaching car lit the interior for a moment – enough to see that the upholstery in front of him was blue – then everything went dark as the car passed. He could hear his dog panting. He felt a distinct metal hardness – a point – cold in the nape hair of his neck.

"If you so much as move a muscle I'll kill you. I will," said the gunman. His voice sounded as if it were shaking with nerves. "Right-oh driver."

"What about the dog?" said the driver.

"What about it? It'd run home. Start yapping, maybe. People'd start looking."

"Aye, mebby"

"On you go."

"There's something not right about it. Bringing a dog."

"On you fuckin go."

The car took off, changed gear and cruised – there seemed to be no hurry about it.

"We're from the IRA," said the gunman. "Who are you?"

There was a silence. He was incapable of answering.

"What's your name?"

He cleared his throat and made a noise. Then said, "John."

"John who?"

"John Shields."

"What sort of name is that?"

It was hard to shrug in the position he was in. He had one foot on either side of the ridge covering the main drive shaft. They were now in an area of street lighting and he saw a Juicy Fruit chewing-gum paper under the driver's seat. What was he playing detective for? The car would be stolen anyway. His hands could touch the floor but were around his knees. He still had the dog's lead wrapped round his fist.

"Any other names?"

"What like?"

"A middle name."

The dog had settled and curled up on the seat beside him. There was an occasional bumping sound as his tail wagged. The gunman wore Doc Martens and stone washed denims.

"I said any other names?"

"No."

"You're lying in your teeth. Not even a Confirmation name?"

"No."

"What school did you go to?"

There was a long pause.

"It's none of your business." There was a sudden staggering pain in the back of his head and he thought he'd been shot. "Aww – for fuck's sake." The words had come from him so he couldn't be dead. The bastard must have hit him with the butt of the gun.

"No cheek," said the gunman. "This is serious."

"For fuck's sake, mate – take it easy." He was shouting and groaning and rubbing the back of his head. The anger in his voice raised the dog and it began to growl. His fingers were slippery. The blow must have broken the skin.

"Let me make myself clear," said the gunman. "I'll come to it in one. Are you a Protestant or a Roman

"Do you have anything that involves killing people?"

Catholic?"

There was a long pause. John pretended to concentrate on the back of his neck.

"That really fuckin hurt."

"I'll ask you again. Are you a Protestant or a Roman Catholic?"

"I'm ... I don't believe in any of that crap. I suppose I'm nothing."

"You're a fuckin wanker – if you ask me."

John protected his neck with his hands thinking he was going to be hit again. But nothing happened.

"What was your parents?"

"The same. In our house nobody believed in anything."

The car slowed and went down the gears. The driver indicated and John heard the rhythmic clinking as it flashed. This must be the Lisburn Road. A main road. This was happening on a main road in Belfast. They'd be heading for the Falls. Some Republican safe house. The driver spoke over his shoulder.

"Let's hear you say the alphabet."

"Are you serious?"

"Yeah – say your abc's for us," said the gunman.

"This is so fuckin ridiculous," said John. He steeled himself for another blow.

"Say it – or I'll kill you." John knew the myth that Protestants and Catholics because of the separate schooling, pronounced the eighth letter of the alphabet differently. But he couldn't remember who said which.

"Eh ... bee ... cee, dee, ee ... eff." He said it very slowly, hoping the right pronunciation would come to him. He stopped.

"Keep going."

"Gee ..." John dropped his voice, "... aitch, haitch ... aye jay kay."

"We have a real smart Alec here," said the gunman. The driver spoke again.

"Stop fuckin about and ask him if he knows anybody in the IRA who can vouch for him."

"Well" said the gunman. "Do you?"

There was another long pause. The muzzle of the gun touched his neck. Pressure was applied to the top bone of his vertebrae.

"Do you?"

"I'm thinking."

"It's not fuckin Mastermind. Do you know anybody in the Provos? Answer me now or I'll blow the fuckin head off you."

"No," John shouted. "There's a couple of guys in work who are Roman Catholics – but there's no way they're Provos."

"Where do you work?"

"The Gas Board."

"A meter man?"

"No. I'm an E.O."

"Did you hear that?" said the gunman to the driver.

"Aye."

"There's not too many Fenians in the Gas Board."

"Naw," said the driver. "If there are any they're not E.O. class. I think this is a dud."

"John Shields," said the gunman. "Tell us this. What do you think of us?"

"What do you mean?"

"What do you think of the IRA? The Provos?"

"Catch yourselves on. You have a gun stuck in my neck and you want me to ..."

"Naw – it'd be interesting. Nothing'll happen – no matter what you say. Tell us what you think."

There was silence as the car slowed down and came to a stop. The reflections from the chrome inside the car became red. Traffic lights. John heard the bleeping of a 'cross now' signal. For the benefit of the blind. Like the pimples on the pavement. To let them know where they were.

"Can you say the Hail Mary? To save your bacon?"

"No – I told you I'm not interested in that kind of thing."

The driver said,

"I think he's okay."

"Sure," said the gunman. "But he still hasn't told us what he thinks of us."

John cleared his throat – his voice was trembling.

"I hate the Provos. I hate everything you stand for." There was a pause. "And I hate you for doing this to me."

"Spoken like a man."

The driver said,

"He's no more a Fenian than I am."

"Another one of our persuasion." The gunman sighed with a kind of irritation. The lights changed from orange to green. The car began to move. John heard the indicator clinking again and the driver turned off the main road into darkness. The car stopped and the handbrake was racked on. The gunman said,

"Listen to me. Careful. It's like in the fairy tale. If you look at us you're dead."

"You never met us," said the driver.

"And if you look at the car we'll come back and kill you – no matter what side you're from. Is that clear? Get out."

Info

An Irish – Northern Irish Chronology

1171 Claiming permission from the Pope, Henry II of England begins conquest of Ireland.

1601 Ulster is divided into shires, English law is introduced, and Gaelic inhabitants are driven off their land which is resettled by Protestant Scots and Englishmen (the plantation of Ulster).

1603 Hugh O'Neill, the leader of the Gaelic population, finally surrenders to English authority.

1649 Oliver Cromwell arrives in Ireland with the New Model Army, the army of the victorious English parliamentarian party of the English Civil War. Three thousand people are killed in his attempt to bring the whole country to Protestantism.

1685 James II, the Catholic brother of Charles II, succeeds to the throne of England. Catholics in Ireland hope for a restoration of their lands.

1689 In the Glorious Revolution James II is deposed and replaced by William III of Orange. James II leads an army to Ulster and lays seige to the town of Derry. It resists for 105 days and is finally relieved by the arrival of William's army.

1690 William himself arrives in Ireland to meet James and his army at the Battle of the Boyne on 1 July. James is defeated in perhaps the most important battle in Irish history. Catholics are now demoted to second-class citizens.

1791 Founding of the Society of United Irishmen, which under the leadership of Wolfe Tone, seeks to make Ireland a republic and break the connection with England.

Celtic figure

1795 Formation of the Orange Order by Protestants.

1798 Insurrection of Tone's United Irishmen, which is brutally suppressed.

1801 Act of Union: the Dublin parliament disappears and Ireland becomes an integral part of the United Kingdom of Great Britain and Ireland.

1858 Founding of the Irish Republican Brotherhood, also known as the Fenians, a militant republican organisation.

1912 Home Rule Bill for Ireland. Vehemently opposed by Ulster Protestants.

1919 War of Independence, lasting two years, starts in Ireland, led by Michael Collins. The British respond by using armed and undisciplined auxiliary policemen known as the Black and Tans, who terrorise the civilian population.

1921 The Anglo-Irish treaty gives independence to the Republic of Ireland (the southern 26 counties) and establishes a separate parliament at Stormont for the six counties of Northern Ireland.

1968 A civil rights movement is set up to improve the situation of the Catholic population. A civil rights march in Londonderry is brutally put down by the police, with 88 people injured.

1969 The British Army is sent to Northern Ireland after disturbances between Protestants and Catholics.

1970 The IRA is re-formed and starts its terror campaign. The IRA splits into the Provisionals or Provos, who favour a military terrorist campaign, and the Officials, who favour a political approach (see glossary p. 50).

1971 Internment or prison without trial for suspected terrorists is introduced.

1972 "Bloody Sunday"; British soldiers kill 14 unarmed civil rights marchers in Londonderry. The Northern Irish parliament at Stormont is abolished and direct rule by the British government is introduced.

1981 Ten IRA prisoners die on hunger strike while demanding political status.

1981 The IRA takes a political as well as a military approach. Its political arm Sinn Fein re-emerges and a Sinn Fein candidate wins the West Belfast seat in the 1983 general election.

1997 Ceasefire by the IRA.

1998 The Good Friday agreement (see glossary p. 50).

1998 Referendums in Northern Ireland and the Irish Republic support the Good Friday agreement.

1998 The Northern Ireland assembly is set up under first minister, David Trimble.

1998 The 1998 Nobel Peace Prize is awarded to David Trimble MP, leader of the Ulster Unionist Party and to John Hume MP, leader of the Social Democratic and Labour Party, for their efforts to find a peaceful solution to the conflict in Northern Ireland.

Study Aids

Abbreviations

n.	=	noun	esp.	=	especially
v.	=	verb	poet.	=	poetical(ly)
adj.	=	adjective	s.o.	=	someone
adv.	=	adverb	s.th.	=	something
prep.	=	preposition	o.s.	=	oneself
conj.	=	conjunction	i.e.	=	that is
sing.	=	singular	l.	=	line
pl.	=	plural	ll.	=	lines
BrE	=	British English	p.	=	page
AmE	=	American English	pp.	=	pages
sl.	=	slang	f.	=	and the following (page, line etc.)
dial.	=	dialect	ff.	=	and the following (pages, lines etc.)
inf.	=	informal	e.g.	=	for example
intro	=	introduction			

The phonetic transcriptions follow the *Longman Dictionary of Contemporary English (DCE)* and J. C. Wells, *Longman Pronunciation Dictionary*.

Cover / Title Page

National Symbols

Each of the nations of Britain has its own symbols, emblems and flags, which are all powerful indications of their separate national identities. England, Scotland, Wales and Ireland all have their own patron saints, who are believed to give special protection to these particular countries.

England's patron saint, St George, is thought to have come from the shores of the Adriatic Sea and was one of a number of legendary Christian saints who killed dragons in the Middle East. St George's Day is 23 April.

St David, the patron saint of Wales, was a sixth century monk and his day, 1 March, is the country's unofficial holiday. The patron saint of Ireland, St Patrick, was one of the country's most important missionaries. He was born in Britain, the son of a Romanised Briton in 372 AD. He was captured by Irish raiders, taken to Ireland and sold into slavery. After six years he escaped and returned to Britain where he became a priest and later a bishop. He then went back to Ireland to spread the Christian faith, mainly in the North of Ireland, in central and eastern Ulster. He is supposed to have rid Ireland of snakes, to have made the blind see and to have raised the dead. St Patrick's Day, 17 March is celebrated by Irish people throughout the world.

St Andrew, the patron saint of Scotland, was a fisherman and one of Jesus' twelve apostles. He was crucified in 60 AD on a cross like an X. This type of cross was named after him and is used on Scotland's national flag, a white diagonal cross on a blue background. St. Andrew's Day is 30 November.

England's flag, a red cross on a white background, is also named after its patron saint St George. In the 1950s separate flags came into use in Wales and Northern Ireland. The Welsh flag shows the Welsh national animal, the red dragon, on a green and white background. The flag of Northern Ireland is the red cross of St George on a white background. At the centre of the cross is a six pointed star - one point for each of the counties of Northern Ireland. Above it is the British crown. In the middle of the star is the red hand of Ulster. A legend tells how the English king said that whoever touched Ireland first would possess the territory. O'Neill, the first Gaelic lord of Ulster, seeing another boat about to reach the Ulster shore before his own, cut off his hand and threw it on the shore to make his claim.

When in 1603 James VI of Scotland became James I of England, and so uniting the two monarchies, a new flag was needed for the royal warships. For some two hundred years English soldiers had displayed the cross of St George on their coats and flags and Scottish soldiers had flown the cross of St Andrew. The two were therefore combined to form the basis of the present flag. This remained in use until 1801 when Ireland was brought into the union. A diagonal red cross of St Patrick was designed and this was added to the flag, which was called the Union Flag or Union Jack. The term "jack" had for a long time been the name for any type of flag on ships. Its origins probably date back to when a sailor was known as a "Jack Tar". Even though the Irish Republic has left the union, the flag remains the same.

Other emblems and animals adopted by each of the countries are: the rose and lion for England, the unicorn and thistle for Scotland, and the leek and daffodil for Wales. Since the union of the Scottish and English monarchies in 1603, the lion of England and unicorn of Scotland have appeared on the royal coat of arms holding the monarch's shield. The national emblem of the Republic of Ireland is the shamrock and its national flag is the green white and orange tricolor.

1 | Rudyard Kipling "The Anvil"

(Joseph) Rudyard Kipling (1865-1936), British novelist, short-story writer and poet, was born in India. He won the Nobel prize for literature in 1907. He is known for his children's stories *The Jungle Book* (1894), and the *Just So Stories* (1902), and the poems *If* and *Gunga Din*.

Vocabulary

1 anvil (n.): a heavy iron block on which pieces of metal are shaped using a hammer - **3 blacksmith** (n.): s.o. who makes and repairs things made of iron, esp. horseshoes - **8 foe** (n.): enemy

Explanations

2 Severn: a river in east Wales and southwest England. It rises in central Wales, flows northeast into England, then southwest to its mouth in the Bristol Channel. It is the longest river in Great Britain with a length of 290 km. - **2 Tyne**: a river in northeast England. It flows eastwards, entering the North Sea at Tynemouth. It is 48 km long. - **3 Norman King**: William I (?1027-87), reigned 1066-87, the first Norman king of England; known as William the Conqueror (see glossary p. 51). - **8 Kingdoms**: the Saxon kingdoms or earldoms that were destroyed by the Normans (see glossary p. 50). At the time of the conquest England consisted of four main earldoms: Northumbria, in the northeast, East Anglia, in the east, Mercia in the west Midlands, and Wessex in the south and southwest. These earldoms were what remained of the Saxon kingdoms that had been united under Alfred the Great (849-899), who

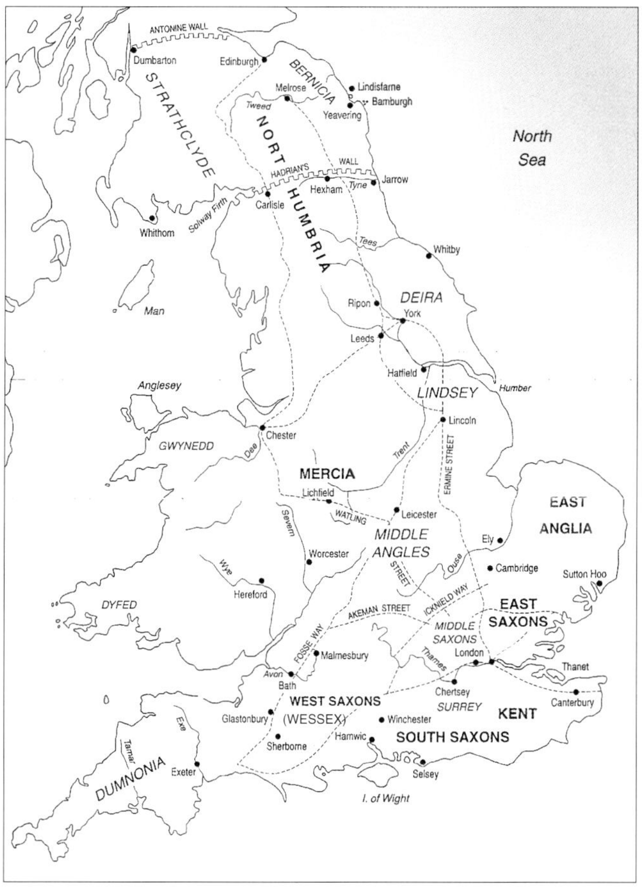

The ancient Saxon kingdoms in the seventh and eighth centuries

Present-day English regions

Awareness

1 What do you know about the Norman Conquest of England in 1066, William the Conqueror, the Normans and the defeated Saxons?

Comprehension

2 Each stanza of the poem describes one particular effect of the Norman Conquest. Describe them in your own words.

Analysis

3 Comment on the effect of the 'anvil' imagery used in the poem. Include in your analysis the images of the hammer, the blacksmith and England as the object on the anvil.
4 At first glance the imagery of "England's on the anvil" (l. 1) might seem negative. What positive effects of this process does the narrator see?
5 Comment on the implications of the description of the Norman king as "our" (l. 3) king.
6 How does the form of the poem reflect and reinforce its content?

Projects

7 Find out whether William the Conqueror's claim to the English throne was justified or not.
8 The effects of the Norman Conquest are presented in this poem in the form of poetic imagery. Find out how the Conquest actually affected the Saxon population of England.
9 Compare the map of the Saxon kingdoms with the map of the English regions. What similarities and differences can you find between the ancient Saxon kingdoms and the present-day English regions? Find out which counties have names which refer to the Anglo Saxons.

2 | Bernard Crick
"An Englishman's Passport"

Bernard Crick (1929-) is Emeritus Professor of Politics at Birkbeck College, London and the author of a number of books, including *In Defence of Politics* (Harmondsworth: Penguin, 1993) and *George Orwell: A Life* (London: Secker and Warburg, 1980).

Vocabulary

1 colloquial (adj.): language or words that are used mainly in conversation rather than in writing or formal speech - **4 existential** (adj.): connected with the existence of humans - **11 overwhelming** (adj.): very large number - **13 suspicion** (n.): feeling that s.o. has done s.th. wrong - **14 assertion** (n.): s.th. that you say or write that you strongly believe - **25 circulation** (n.): number of copies of a newspaper, magazine or book that are usually sold each day, week, month, etc. - **26 bizarrely** (adv.): very unusually or strangely - **31 preface** (n.): /ˈprefəs/ an introduction at the beginning of a book - **36 to comprise** (v.): to consist of - **42 mainland** (n.): here: the largest island of the British Isles - **46 archipelago** (n.): /ˌɑːkɪˈpeləgəʊ/ a group of islands - **52 question-begging** (adj.): discussing s.th. in a way that makes it seem that a fact is definitely true when in fact it may not be - **52 pre-emptive** (adj.): done to harm s.o. before they can harm you - **55 entity** (n.): s.th. that exists as a single and complete unit - **56 to proclaim** (v.): to say publicly that s.th. important is true or exists - **62 device** (n.): here: a plan or trick

Explanations

2 United Kingdom of Great Britain and [Northern] Ireland: Before 1922, when the Republic of Ireland was created, British passports referred to The United Kingdom of Great Britain and Ireland. They now refer to The United Kingdom of Great Britain and Northern Ireland. - **12 UK**: the short form of United Kingdom of Great Britain and Northern Ireland - **21 Central Office of Information or C.O.I.**: a government agency which obtains and distributes information for government departments and ministries - **44 *O.E.D.***: *Oxford English Dictionary* - **50 Empire**: Up to the end of the Second World War (1939-45) it was common usage for all inhabitants of all the territories of the British Empire to call themselves British. This usage declined and ended with increasingly restrictive immigration policies by successive British governments.

Awareness

1 Make short notes on what you understand to be the difference (if any) between England, Britain, Great Britain, the British Isles, and the United Kingdom.

Comprehension

2 Why are many English people confused when they have to give their nationality?
3 What are the possible meanings of a) 'Britain' and b) 'Great Britain' in the text? Explain the difference in usage in the C.O.I. book *Britain*, the *O.E.D.*, and Crick's own.
4 Why does Crick think it is 'bizarre' to refer to the United Kingdom as 'Britain'?
5 What is the significance of the use of the terms 'Britain' and 'Great Britain' for Northern Ireland Loyalists?

Analysis

6 How do the English on the one hand and the Welsh, Scots, and Irish on the other differ in the way they view the words referring to their nationality?
7 What arguments are the examples quoted by Crick (the passport, the C.O.I. book *Britain* and the *O.E.D.*) intended to support?
8 What does this article tell us about the nature of the national identity of the British?

Opinion

9 What significance does Crick's discussion of British identity have for other nations (e.g. Germany, France, Spain, the United States, ex-Yugoslavia, ex-Soviet Union)?

Project

10 Investigate and compare the definitions given in dictionaries and books on the English usage of the terms 'Britain' and 'Great Britain'.
11 Investigate the history of the United Kingdom and the development of a British identity.

3 Stanley Baldwin
"England Is the Country, and the Country Is England"

Stanley Baldwin (1867-1947) was prime minister of Britain three times (1923-24, 1924-29 and 1935-37). He was a member of the Conservative Party and saw himself as a typical representative of Middle England, by which he meant both middle class England and a politically moderate England. After his retirement from the premiership he became Earl Baldwin of Bewdley.

Vocabulary

9 substitution (n.): s.th. you use instead of the thing you would usually use - **10 Dinner-book** (n.): (also dinner book) a book which is used at special dinners in which people write comments - **19 gallant** (adj.): brave - **23 stock** (n.): a particular type or group of people - **25 contradictory** (adj.): (of two statements or beliefs) unable to be both true; incompatible, inconsistent - **31 chronicler** (n.): s.o. who describes a series of events in the order in which they happen - **32 aping** (n.): copying - **32 ancestor** (n.): a member of your family or nation who lived a long time ago - **33 prey** (n.): here: s.o. who suffers s.th. unpleasant - **39 emergency** (n.): an unexpected and dangerous situation that must be dealt with immediately - **39 serene** (adj.): calm, relaxed - **40 indifferent** (adj.): not caring about what is happening - **41 to heed** (v.): to pay attention to s.th. - **43 ruthless** (adj.): so determined to get what you want that you do not care if you have to hurt other people in order to do it - **51 under-dog** (n.): (now: underdog) a person that is weak and is always treated badly - **57 immortal** (adj.): living or continuing forever - **59 to mint** (v.): to make a coin - **62 gross** (adj.): /grəʊs/ extreme, unacceptable - **62 vice** (n.): a bad or immoral quality in s.o.'s character - **63 ills** (n.): problems and difficulties - **63 fortune** (n.): chance - **75 to steam-roller** (v.): (now: steamroller) to crush or destroy

Explanations

14 ff. 'For in spite of ...' from the opera *H.M.S. Pinafore* (1878) by Sir W(illiam) S(chwenck) Gilbert (1836-1911) and Sir Arthur Sullivan (1842-1900) - **17 Patron Saint**: (also patron saint) a Christian saint (= very holy person) who is believed to give special protection to a particular place, activity, or person - **19 St. George**: saint and martyr, died ?303, according to legend the killer of a dragon in Libya (see also the text "National Symbols", p. 28) - **20 Adriatic**: the Adriatic Sea, situated between Italy and the Dalmatian coast - **33 William the Norman**: also William I and William the Conqueror; ?1027-87; duke of Normandy (1035-87) and king of England (1066-87) (see glossary p. 51) - **55 war**: here: the First World War (1914-18) - **56 Ruskin**: John (1819-1900), English art critic and social reformer. Later in life he argued for social and economic planning. - **69 Charles Dickens**: (1812-70), English novelist, famous for the humour and sympathy of his characterisation and his criticism of social injustice

Awareness

1 Write down those characteristics that you think of as being 'typically English' and 'typically German'. Compare your notes with those of other students. What do you agree and disagree on? Why?

Comprehension

2 What are the characteristics that Baldwin considers to be typically English?

Analysis

3 What is the significance of Baldwin's mentioning of God with reference to English qualities? (ll. 10, 29)

4 What effect do you think Baldwin's speech would have had on his audience? Indicate how the structure of the speech, the rhetorical means used and his argumentation achieve this.

Opinion

5 Do you think that the substitution of 'Britain' for 'England' and 'Briton' for 'Englishman' would ruin the most beautiful passages in the English language?

6 From l. 38 to the end of the text substitute the word 'German', 'Germans' or 'Germany' for those of "Englishman", "English" or "England". What effect do these changes have on you and what effect might the speech have on a German audience?

7 Write a letter to Stanley Baldwin in which you give your opinion on the ideas expressed in his speech.

Project

8 Investigate other writers' opinions on the nature of Englishness. Some well-known texts on this topic are: George Orwell, "The English People" in *The Collected Essays, Journalism and Letters of George Orwell. Volume 3: As I Please. 1943-1945.* Ed. Sonia Orwell and Ian Angus (Harmondsworth: Penguin, 1970) pp. 15-55; J. B. Priestley, *English Journey* (London: Heinemann, 1949 and Harmondsworth: Penguin, 1986); Ernest Barker, *The Character of England* (Oxford: Clarendon, 1947); Ernest Barker, *Britain and the British People* (London: Oxford University Press, 1958); Jeremy Paxman, *The English: A Portrait of a People* (Harmondsworth: Penguin, 1999).

4 | Peter Hetherington
"Ashington: A Shared Name but Miles Apart"

Vocabulary

5 to be poles apart: to be as different from each other as it is possible to be - **7 stuck** (adj.): here: situated - **9 solicitor** (n.): a type of lawyer in Britain who gives advice, does the necessary work when property is bought and sold, and defends people, esp. in the lower courts of law - **10 to chair** (v.): to be the chairperson of a meeting - **10 parish council** (n.): a group of people who are responsible for taking decisions about a small area, esp. a village - **12 cradle** (n.): here: most central part - **16 councillor** (n.): member of a council, the organisation that is responsible for local government in a particular district or region of Britain - **18 colliery** (adj.): mining - **22 pit** (n.): coal mine - **25 well-heeled** (adj.): rich - **26 down-at-heel** (adj.): appearing to be poor; shabby - **30 to forge links** (v.): to develop a strong relationship - **30 twinning** (n.): forming a relationship between two towns, usually but not always, in different countries - **31 to debunk** (v.): to show that s.o.'s ideas or beliefs are false - **41 to stumble across** (v.): to discover s.th. by chance - **47 liaison** (adj.): /lɪˈeɪzən/ - **51 to underestimate** (v.): to think s.th. is less important than it is - **53 stark** (adj.): unpleasantly clear and impossible to avoid; harsh - **64 dingy** (adj.): /ˈdɪndʒɪ/ dark, dirty and in bad condition (of a room, street or place only) - **67 hilarious** (adj.): extremely funny - **68 launch** (n.): here: start - **73 lecturer** (n.): s.o. who has the lowest teaching rank at a British university or college - **75 commuter belt** (n.): an area around a large city from which many people travel to work every day - **76 brown ale** (n.): dark mild beer sold in bottles - **76 to swill** (v.): to drink s.th. in large amounts - **77 pitman** (n.): coalminer - **80 emerging** (adj.): beginning, appearing - **92 to get on** (v.): to have a friendly relationship - **93 handout** (n.): money or goods given to s.o., for example because they are poor - **94 to wince** (v.): to suddenly feel very uncomfortable or embarrassed because, for example, of s.th. that happens or is said. - ***chart* semi** (n.): semi-detached house; a house that is joined to another house by one shared wall - ***chart* constituency** (n.): an area of the country that elects an MP to parliament

Explanations

11 West Sussex: a county to the south of London - **12 Weald**: a region of southeast England, south of London in the counties of Kent, Surrey, East and West Sussex - **14 Watford**: a town in southeast England just north of London. For some people who live in the southeast of England it is humorously considered to be on the most northerly boundary of that region of England. - **27 Northumberland**: a county in northeast England, on the Scottish border - **28 Workers' Educational Association**: (also WEA) an organisation with the aim of improving educational standards among working people; founded in 1903 by Albert Mansbridge (1876-1952) - **31 Disraeli**: Benjamin, 1st Earl of Beaconsfield (1804-81), British Conservative statesman, prime minister 1868 and 1874-80. He ensured that Britain bought a controlling interest in the Suez Canal (1875) and made Queen Victoria Empress of India. In his novels *Coningsby* (1844) and *Sybil, or the Two Nations* (1845) he pointed out divisions between the poor and the rich in British society. - **32 "Two nations ..."**: the quotation is taken from Disraeli's novel *Sybil, or the Two Nations*. The quotation is, however, being misused here, since it does not refer to the divisions between the north and south of England, but to the division between rich and poor. The full quotation is:

"Well, society may be in its infancy," said Egremont, slightly smiling; "but, say what you like, our Queen reigns over the greatest nation that ever existed."

"'Which nation?" asked the young stranger, "for she reigns over two."

The stranger paused; Egremont was silent, but looked enquiringly.

"Yes," resumed the young stranger after a moment's interval. "Two nations; between whom there is no intercourse and no sympathy; who are as ignorant of each other's habits, thoughts and feelings, as if they were dwellers in different zones, or inhabitants of different planets; who are formed by different breeding, are fed by different food, are ordered by different manners, and are not governed by the same laws."

"You speak of – " said Egremont, hesitatingly.

"THE RICH AND THE POOR."[1]

- **40 community worker**: a person who works among the people of a particular area in order to help them - **42 A24**: the main road between London and Worthing on which Ashington, West Sussex is situated. All important main roads in Britain, apart from motorways, have the prefix A and are known as A-roads. - **43 Worthing**: a seaside town in West Sussex, population 92,050 (1980) - **43 Horsham**: a small town in West Sussex, north of Worthing - **81 National Curriculum:** a programme of study at schools that is intended to make sure that standards and contents of subjects are uniform throughout Britain - **89 Tory**: a member of the Conservative Party - ***chart* council housing**: houses and flats provided by the local council for a low rent

Awareness

1 Using the two pictures of the signposts on p. 5, imagine what the two towns of Ashington might be like. Looking at the cartoon, what attitudes do you imagine it tries to illustrate?

Comprehension

2 What are the main differences between the two Ashingtons according to the text?
3 How did the link between the two towns come about?
4 What advantages arising from the twinning arrangement are mentioned in the article?

Analysis

5 What opinions and stereotypes do the inhabitants of each of the Ashingtons have about the other?
6 Consider how far the people presented in the article confirm or contradict the stereotypes and opinions you found in question 5.
7 What potential for conflict between the two towns can you find in the article?

Opinion

8 Imagine you are a local councillor in one of the two Ashingtons. Write a speech to be given at a council meeting in which you support or reject the twinning arrangement with the other town.
9 How far does the article confirm the statement about the north and south of England: 'Two nations, between whom there is no [...] sympathy; who are as ignorant of each other's habits, thoughts and feelings, as if they were dwellers in different zones, or inhabitants of different planets.' (ll. 32ff.)

Projects

10 Imagine that you are from one of the two Ashingtons and have taken part in an exchange with the other. Write a short account of your experiences and feelings.
11 Find out about the reasons for the north-south divide in England.

[1] Benjamin Disraeli, *Sybil, or The Two Nations* (London: Oxford University Press), 1970, p. 67.

5 | John C. McIntyre
The Empty Highlands

John McIntyre (1941-   ) was born in Lanarkshire in the Central Belt of Scotland and is a lecturer in Spanish and Latin American Studies at the University of Strathclyde.

Vocabulary

2 rugged (adj.): /ˈrʌgɪd/ rough and uneven - **3 stand** (n.): here: group of trees in a forest - **6 loch** (n.): /lɒx/ (Scottish English) a lake or part of the sea partly enclosed by land - **10 glen** (n.): a deep narrow valley in Scotland or Ireland - **12 'neath** (prep.) - (poetic) below, beneath - **12 glowering** (adj.): looking angrily - **12 ben** (n.): (Scottish English) mountain - **18 osprey** (n.): a type of large bird that eats fish - **18 to swoop** (v.): to move suddenly and steeply down through the air - **18 to slay** (v.): to kill - **20 prey** (n.): an animal that is hunted and killed by another animal - **21 stag** (n.): a fully grown male deer (= an animal with large branching horns) - **22 to lock** (v.): to join tightly together - **26 to betray** (v.): to be disloyal to s.o. who trusts you so that they are harmed or upset - **26 kin** (n.): family - **27 laird** (n.): /leəd/ a Scottish landowner - **29 peasant** (n.): /peznt/ s.o. in a poor country who does farm work on the piece of land on which they live - **33 famed** (adj.): (poetic) well-known

Explanations

Title **Highlands**: a mountainous region of northern Scotland, north of a line between Dumbarton on the Firth of Clyde and Stonehaven on the East Coast, but excluding the flat areas around Aberdeen - **1 Alba**: the Gaelic name for Scotland; a united kingdom of Picts and Scots, known as Albyn or Alba was proclaimed under the Scots' king Kenneth MacAlpine in 844 - **3 Sitka**: Sitka spruce; a type of North American pinetree which is grown for its valuable wood; since 1919 when it was set up the Forestry Commission, a government organisation, has encouraged the planting of forests in Britain. Its programme of covering vast areas of the Scottish highlands with Sitka spruce has been particularly controversial. The Forestry Commission is now making efforts to replace the Sitka spruce monoculture with a wider variety of trees. - **25 chiefs**: the heads of the Scottish clans

Awareness
1 Make brief notes on what you know about Scotland. Compare your notes with those of other students.

Comprehension
2 Why are the Highlands empty?
3 What resources do the Highlands have?
4 What is the significance of the phrase "if so we dare" (l. 40)?

Analysis
5 What do the scenes depicting the Highlands tell us about the speaker's view of this region?
6 Explain why the speaker "asks himself in wonder" (ll. 7, 15) why the Highlands are empty.
7 What features of the text would lead you to think that it was written as a song (to be heard) and not as a poem (to be read)?

Opinion
8 What effect did this poem have on you? Explain what images and words created this effect.
9 Who might the "I" of the poem be?

Project
10 Find out about the Highland Clearances. Write a report, with illustrations and maps, on this important period in Scottish history.

6 | Tom Leonard
"This Is Thi Six A Clock News"

Tom Leonard was born in Glasgow in 1944. He was educated in Glasgow and took an MA at Glasgow University. The collection of poems *Six Glasgow Poems* and *A Priest Came on at Merkland Street* established him as an original writer whose innovation was the serious use of working class Glasgow speech in literary texts.

Vocabulary

15 scruff (n.): s.o. who looks untidy or dirty - **38 to belt up** (v.): to be quiet

Explanations

cartoon: Och aye /ɒx aɪ/: (dial.) Oh yes - **7 BBC**: British Broadcasting Corporation; a public corporation (= body) for radio and television broadcasting in Britain. It is financed by the sale of television viewing licences and not by advertising. - **7 BBC accent**: also known as Received Pronunciation or RP; it is the accent used by newsreaders on the BBC and is considered by some people to be the standard for spoken English. Others think it is the accent of privilege imposed on the nation by a large London-based state institution. (See glossary pp. 49, 51) - **9 widny**: (dial.) wouldn't - **12 wia**: (dial.) with a - **16 toktaboot**: (dial.) talked about - **32 yoouz**: (dial.) youse; you (plural) - **34 yirsellz**: (dial.) yourselves - **35 canny**: (dial.) can't

Awareness

1 Why is the news always read in the standard dialect and accent (see glossary pp. 49f. for the difference between accent and dialect) and never read in a regional accent even when this would be comprehensible to all listeners?

Comprehension

2 Translate the poem into Standard English. Explain how the change in language changes the impact of the poem. Look at the info on "Eye Dialect" below.

Analysis

3 Using the info on "Eye Dialect" below, indicate the ways in which Tom Leonard represents the Glasgow dialect in the areas of accent, vocabulary and grammar. Are there any inconsistencies?
4 How does the poem show the arrogance of speakers who have what is called a BBC accent?
5 How does the poem express the resentment of those people who have regional accents?

Opinion

6 Write a letter to Tom Leonard in which you either a) support his ideas and make suggestions for improving the status of regional and social accents and dialects or b) criticise his ideas as expressed in the poem, pointing out the advantages of a standard accent and dialect.

Projects

7 Listen to some programmes on BBC radio or television (via some satellite and cable transmissions and also via long wave) and try to distinguish between the different accents used.
8 Find out how RP came to be the dominant accent in British public life.

Info

Eye Dialect

Eye dialect is the attempt by writers to suggest a character's social class or regional origin by means of non-standard spelling. This type of writing is designed just to give an impression of the dialect concerned and may not be phonologically correct in a number of ways.

The representation of dialect and accent is therefore a simplification of the language in question and is usually carried out using a very small number of key sound-spelling features which are easy to represent in writing.

Info

They are:
- dropping letter(s) at the ends of words, e.g. 'an' for 'and', 'nothin' for 'nothing'
- dropping letter(s) at the beginnings of words, e.g. 'orse' for 'horse'
  (In these two cases an apostrophe is sometimes, but not always substituted for the missing letters.)
- assimilating spellings to match assimilating pronunciations, e.g. 'wanna' for 'want to', 'gonna' for 'going to'
- using common abbreviations, e.g. 'cos' or 'coz' for 'because'
- using conventionalised spellings which suggest a regional or social accent but which are not phonetically different from the standard pronunciation, e.g. 'woz' for 'was' (to suggest Cockney speech), 'yeah' for 'yes', 'ya' for 'you' (to suggest colloquial speech)
- using spellings which suggest a regional or social accent and which are phonetically different from the standard pronunciation, e.g. 'doan' for 'don't', 'feller' for 'fellow', 'drarp' for 'drop', 'I-talian' or 'eye-talian' for 'Italian'.

In addition to the above writers often include:

syntactic features
- nonstandard tense forms, e.g. 'we was' for 'we were'
- nonstandard determiners, e.g. 'me' for 'my', 'yous' for 'you' (plural)
- nonstandard use of modal verbs, e.g. 'he hadn't ought to have' for 'he ought not to have'
- nonstandard use of prepositions, e.g. 'off of' for 'of'
- use of multiple negation, e.g. 'he don't know nothing' for 'he doesn't know anything'
- nonstandard agreement, e.g. 'there's a lot of people' for 'there are a lot of people'.

7 | Billy Wolfe
"The Case for Scottish Independence"*

Billy (William Cuthbertson) Wolfe (1924-) has been a member of the National Council of the Scottish National Party since 1991.

Vocabulary

1 to link (v.): to connect, join - **6 alienation** (n.): the feeling of not being a part of society or a group - **11 bent on** (adj.): completely determined to do s.th. - **12 to promote** (v.): to help s.th. to develop and be successful - **12 habitual** (adj.): usual, typical - **18 current affairs** (n.): important political events that are happening now - **19 dole queue** (n.): line of unemployed people waiting to collect their money from the government - **27 to avert** (v.): to prevent s.th. unpleasant from happening - **36 to hack about** (v.): to cut s.th. into pieces or cut pieces off s.th. - **38 to prescribe** (v.): to say what medicine or treatment a sick person should have - **47 inaugural** (adj.): the first speech given by s.o. starting an important job - **47 address** (n.): a formal speech - **52 alien** (adj.): foreign - **54 proviso** (n.): a condition that you ask for before you will agree to s.th.

Explanations

11 infant classes: classes in a school for children aged 5 to 7 years - **12 one nation theory**: the theory that England, Wales and Scotland form one nation, Britain - **32 deep water facilities**: buildings and equipment which enable large ships to be built - **32 Clyde**: a river in southern Scotland which flows northwest to the Firth of Clyde. The shipyards on its banks were once the shipbuilding centre of the world. There are still extensive shipyards servicing the North Sea oil industry. - **34 Angleterre**: the French word for England; a reference to the widespread and incorrect use in many countries of England to mean Britain (see also Text 2) - **35-36 Quotation**: Philip Guedalla (1889 - 1944) was a popular English writer and historian. His comment refers to the fact that many British Prime Ministers had been Scottish. - **37 Budget Day**: the day, usually in March, on which the government makes an official statement about how much it intends to spend and what taxes will be necessary - **38 Westminster**: here: the British government (from the district in London where parliament is situated) - **41 balance of payments**: the difference between what a country spends in order to buy goods and services abroad and the money it earns selling goods and services abroad - **47 Rector**: the person in charge of a university in Scotland; at Glasgow University the Rector is elected by the students. - **48 James (Jimmy) Reid**: a Communist shop steward in a Glasgow shipyard; he became a national figure in the 1970s when he led campaigns against the closing of shipyards in Scotland.

Awareness

1 Work out reasons why Scotland might wish to be an independent nation.

Comprehension

2 List the ways in which, according to Wolfe, Scotland suffers because of its link with England.

Analysis

3 Explain what you think Wolfe means by "alienation".
4 In what ways would Scotland benefit from being independent from England?
5 What rhetorical means does Wolfe use in order to underline his message? Examine the arguments and how they are structured, the tone and language used, and their effect on the reader.

Opinion

6 Give your own opinion on the views expressed in this extract.
7 Write a reply to Wolfe's views by a Scot who wishes to remain united with England.

Project

8 Investigate the choices open to Scotland: union with England; devolution; and independence. Find out and summarise the views on these issues of the main political parties: Labour, Conservative, Liberal Democrat, and Scottish National Party.

8 | Niall Ferguson

"As a Scot and a Briton I Fear Today for Our Future"

Niall Ferguson is Tutor in history at Jesus College, Cambridge and author of a number of books on British and European history.

Vocabulary

12 kilt (n.): a type of thick skirt worn by Scottish men - **15 private** (n.): a soldier of the lowest rank - **23 to amount to** (v.): to have the same effect as - **24 repeal** (n.): official ending (of a law) - **32 to avert** (v.): to prevent s.th. unpleasant from happening - **36 crucial** (adj.): /kruːʃəl/ extremely important - **40 to inaugurate** (v.): to come at the beginning (of an important change or period of time) - **41 to underestimate** (v.): to think that s.th. is less important than it is - **41 peril** (n.): danger - **44 to understate** (v.): to describe s.th. in a way that makes it seem less important than it really is - **49 to slumber** (v.): to sleep - **51 half-baked** (adj.): here: not fully developed - **55 unparalleled** (adj.) greater or better than all others - **56 by the same token**: in the same way; for the same reasons - **67 to acclaim** (v.): to praise s.th. or s.o. publicly - **69 at once** (adv.): here: at the same time - **71 craggy** (adj.): having steep cliffs and mountains covered in rough rocks - **75 unqualified** (adj.): here: complete and without any criticism - **81 to dawn on** (v.): to realise, understand s.th. for the first time - **82 writ large** (adj.): in a clearer and stronger form - **88 to repeal** (v.): to officially end a law - **91 mandate** (v.): the right and power of a government to carry out certain policies - **92 drafted** (adj.): written but needing to be changed before having its final form - **94 subsidy** (n.): money that is paid by a government to help people or groups in society - **101 bogus** (adj.): not true or real

Explanations

9 Glasgow Academy: a well known independent grammar school, founded in 1864 - **14 Great War**: another name for the First World War (1914-18) - **15 Seaforth Highlanders**: a regiment of the British Army named after the Earl of Seaforth of the Mackenzie clan, originally formed in 1778; in 1961 it was merged with The Queen's Own Cameron Highlanders to form The Queen's Own Highlanders. - **17 Tony Blair**: (1953-) Anthony Charles Lynton, leader of the Labour Party, and since 1 May 1997 prime minister - **18 devolution**: policy of giving power from a national government to a group or organisation at a local or regional level. See info "Devolution", p. 45. - **20 the Union**: the uniting of the English and Scottish crowns in 1603 and of the English and Scottish parliaments in 1707 - **26 James VI of Scotland**: (1566-1625), son of Mary I, also known as Mary Tudor or Bloody Mary, sister of Elizabeth I, reigned as king of Scotland 1567-1625 and as king of England

and Ireland 1603-25. - **27 Elizabeth I**: (1533-1603), daughter of Henry VIII, queen of England and Ireland 1558-1603 - **28 Tudor**: an English royal family descended from the Welshman Owen Tudor (Welsh *Tewdwr*) (died 1461) - **30 PhD** /piːeɪtʃdiː/: Doctor of Philosophy, from Latin *philosophiae doctor*; a university degree of very high rank, above an MA or MSc - **34 Charles I**: (1600-49) reigned 1625-49; in his conflict with parliament in the English Civil War 1642-49 Charles I was in alliance with the Scots. He and his supporters lost the war and Charles was beheaded (= had his head cut off) in 1649. - **37 Charles Edward Stuart**: (1720-88), son of James Stuart, both of whom claimed the English throne. James was known as the Old Pretender (= claimant to the throne) and Charles was known as the Young Pretender or Bonnie Prince Charlie. (See info "A Scottish Chronology", p. 13) - **38 Lowland**: coming from the Lowlands, a low, generally flat region of Scotland, around the Forth and Clyde valleys - **40 Act of Union**: the parliamentary act (= law) of 1707 by which Scotland was united with England to form Great Britain - **53 Highland**: coming from the Highlands, a mountainous region of northern Scotland, north of a line between Dumbarton on the Firth of Clyde and Stonehaven on the East Coast, but excluding the flat areas around Aberdeen - **54 Jock**: an informal, sometimes insulting word for a Scotsman - **63 James Boswell**: (1740-95), Scottish author, companion and biographer of Samuel Johnson. He is known for *Journal of a Tour to the Hebrides* (1785) and *The Life of Samuel Johnson* (1791). - **64 Samuel Johnson**: (1709-84), English lexicographer, writer, critic, and conversationalist; known as Dr Johnson. A leading figure in the literary London of his day, he is noted for his *Dictionary of the English Language* (1755), edition of *Shakespeare* (1765), and *The Lives of the English Poets* (1777). - **65 Walter Scott**: Sir (1771-1832) Scottish novelist and poet. He established the form of the historical novel in Britain. Notable novels are *Waverley* (1814), *Rob Roy* (1817), *The Heart of Midlothian* (1818), *Ivanhoe* (1819), *Kenilworth* (1821), and *Quentin Durward* (1823). - **65 Thomas Carlyle**: (1795-1881) Scottish essayist, historian and political philosopher. He established his reputation as a historian with his *History of the French Revolution* (1837). - **66 John Buchan**: /ˈbʌkən/ 1st Baron Tweedsmuir (1875-1940), Scottish statesman, historian and novelist; his most notable work is *The Thirty-Nine Steps* (1915). - **74 Alex Salmond**: (Alexander Elliot Sanderoon) (1954-), Scottish National Party MP for the constituency of Banff and Buchan; leader of the Scottish National Party - **74 Scottish National Party**: a political party founded in 1934 which seeks independence for Scotland. In the 1997 general election it won 6 out of 72 Scottish seats. - **75 Yes Yes campaign**: the campaign in the 1997 Devolution Referendum for people to vote yes to both the proposals made: 1) I agree that there should be a Scottish parliament and 2) I agree that a Scottish parliament should have tax varying powers. See also the info on "Devolution", pp. 22, 45. - **81 First Minister**: the title to be given to the leader of the governing party in the Scottish parliament - **82 Strathclyde Regional Council**: a former local government region in west central Scotland covering the densely populated area around Glasgow - **96 Mr Dewar**: Donald; the secretary of state for Scotland from May 1997 until May 1999, and now First Minister of Scotland - **96 Thursday**: All elections and referendums are held on a Thursday in Britain.

Awareness

1 Think of reasons why Scotland would wish to remain within the United Kingdom rather than becoming independent. What message does the cartoon convey in this context?

Comprehension

2 Write out a chronology of the events mentioned in the first half of the article.
3 What reasons does the writer give for saying that a union of crowns is less binding than a union of parliaments?
4 What did Britain gain from having Scotland as part of the United Kingdom?
5 What did Scotland gain from being part of the Union?
6 What criticisms does the writer make of the referendum?

Analysis

7 What is the function of the first paragraph?
8 How is the writer's Scottish and British identity expressed in this article?
9 Why, according to the writer, will demands for independence be strengthened after devolution – the creation of a Scottish parliament?
10 What rhetorical means does the writer use to underline his arguments against devolution?

Opinion

11 Discuss whether devolution should necessarily lead to the break-up of the United Kingdom.
12 Compare the texts by Billy Wolfe and Niall Ferguson. Which one makes the best case? Give reasons for your choice.

Project

13 Find out about how Scotland came to be united with England and how this was received in Scotland.

9 Michael Williams
"Keeping up with the Joneses"

Vocabulary

2 pagan (adj.): (of religious beliefs) not belonging to any of the main religions of the world and possibly coming from a time before these religions - **3 longship** (n.): a long narrow open boat as used by the Vikings - **4 ancestor** (n.): a member of your family who lived a long time ago - **6 derogatory** (adj.): insulting and disapproving - **12 cleansing** (n.): getting rid of s.th. which is not wanted - **21 bewildering** (adj.): confusing - **21 buccaneer** (n.): here: s.o. who succeeds by using any method, including cheating - **22 quest** (n.): long search for s.th. - **22 to acknowledge** (v.): to admit or accept that s.th. is true - **23 predominance** (n.): having power or importance - **31 patron** (n.): s.o. who gives support to a person or organisation - **32 regicide** (n.): /'redʒɪsaɪd/ the crime of killing a king or queen (see Oliver Cromwell below) - **34 rift** (n.): a situation in which two people or groups dislike or distrust each other - **46 bloodstock** (n.): group or family from which other people are descended - **48 stolid** (adj.): not reacting to situations or getting excited by them when most people would react - **49 wordy** (adj.): using too many words - **50 to exemplify** (v.): to be a very typical example of s.th. - **52 angel-tongued** (adj.): able to speak very well and persuasively - **56 to discard** (v.): to get rid of s.th. because it is useless - **60 to charge** (v.): to say publicly that you think s.o. has done s.th. wrong - **69 bailiff** (n.): here: s.o. who looks after a farm or land that belongs to s.o. else - **70 tenant** (n.): s.o. who lives in a house or on land and pays rent to the person who owns it - **72 to snort** (v.): to express anger or annoyance by breathing air noisily through your nose - **73 handle** (n.): (inf.) name - **78 reunion** (n.): a social meeting of people who have not met for a long time - **82 nickname** (n.): a name given to s.o., esp. by their friends or family, that is not their real name - **87 prominent** (adj.): here: large and sticking out - **104 medieval** (adj.): connected with the Middle Ages - **104 undertaker** (n.): s.o. whose job is to arrange burying or burning a dead person - **104 to reel off** (v.): to repeat a lot of information quickly and easily - **106 tribal** (adj.): connected with a group consisting of people of the same race who have the same beliefs, customs, language, etc. - **107 bardic** (adj.): connected with a bard (= a poetic word for poet) - **113 addicted** (adj.): liking to do or have s.th. so much you do not want to stop - **114 keen-witted** (adj.): able to understand things quickly and give quick clever replies - **115 obsessed** (adj.): thinking about s.th. or s.o. all the time - **116 abstemious** (adj.): /əb'stiːmjəs/ careful not to have too much food, drink, etc. - **120 mainstay** (n.): s.o. who does most of the important work for a group or an organisation - **123 to bestride** (v.): (past tense bestrode) to stand over s.th. with one leg on each side of it - **125 humiliation** (n.): a feeling of shame and great embarrassment, because you have been made to look stupid or weak - **127 to jeer** (v.): to laugh unkindly at s.o. to show that you disapprove of them - **128 crepe** (adj.): /kreɪp/ made of light, soft, thin cloth with very small folded lines on the surface - **129 winceyette** (adj.): made of a light material with a soft surface, used esp. for clothes you wear in bed - **135 hideous** (adj.): extremely unpleasant or ugly - **136 scar** (n.): a permanent mark that is left after you have had a cut or wound - **136 to scorch** (v.): to burn s.th. slightly so that its surface changes colour - **137 slate** (adj.): made of dark grey rock that can easily be split into flat thin pieces - **138 to rape** (v.): here: to destroy the environment suddenly and unnecessarily - **140 desolation** (n.): being empty and looking sad because there are no people there - **143 clad** (adj.): (lit.) wearing a particular kind of clothing - **143 samite** (n.): a heavy cloth of silk, often with gold or silver threads - **144 mermaid** (n.): a woman in stories who has a fish's tail instead of legs - **145 split-ends** (n.): a condition of s.o.'s hair in which the ends have split into several parts - **148 bard** (n.): poet

Explanations

2 Saxon: after the Romans left Britain it was invaded by Saxons, Angles and Jutes from northern Europe (see info "A British Chronology", p. 7 and glossary, p. 51) - **2 lager-lout**: a young man who drinks too much and then behaves violently and rudely; here the author is referring to the fact that the inhabitants of Britain at the time of the Anglo-Saxon invasions had a highly developed civilisation and were Christians; the invading Anglo-Saxons were, in comparison, considered uncivilised and barbarous. - **3 Kent**: a county in southeast England where the Angles and Saxons first landed - **4 Briton**: the name given to the inhabitants of Britain when the Romans came; also still used as a formal name for s.o. from Britain (see glossary p. 49) - **5 *Velschen***: cf. German *welsch* and Old English *Wealas*, plural of *Wealh*, a foreigner - **7 *Cymru***: /'kʌmrɪ/ natives or inhabitants of Wales - **11 Teuton**: one of the ancient Germanic peoples of northwestern Europe - **12 Celt**: an ancient European people; the Britons, the original inhabitants of Britain were Celts (see glossary p. 50) - **13 Cornwall**: a county in the southwest of England; its name has the same derivation as that of Wales, in Old English "Cornweals" simply meant "the Welsh in Cornwall" - **13 Cumbria**: a former district and now county in the northwest of England - **16 Brittany**: a region of northwest France - **16 Breton**: name of the language and inhabitant of Brittany - **25 *crachach*** (n.): /kraxax/ Welsh for "snobs" - **30 Chancellor**: (arch.) the chief adviser of the king - **30 Thomas Cromwell**: Earl of Essex ?1485-1540, English statesman - **32 Oliver Cromwell**: 1599-1658, English general and statesman. He led the parliamentary army against the royalists in the English Civil War and was one of those responsible for the killing of King Charles I in 1649. - **38 Evelyn Waugh**: /'iːvlɪn 'wɔː/ 1903-66, English novelist; his earlier satirical works include *Decline and Fall* (1928), *Vile Bodies* (1930), *A Handful of Dust* (1934), and *Scoop* (1938). His later novels include *Brideshead Revisited* (1945), the trilogy *Men at Arms* (1952), *Officers and Gentlemen* (1955) and *Unconditional Surrender* (1961). - **45 Highland**: coming from a mountainous region of northern Scotland, distinguished by Gaelic culture; it was settled mainly by Picts, and Scots from Ireland (see info "A Scottish Chronology", pp. 13f.) - **45 Lowland**: coming from a low generally flat region of Central Scotland around the Forth and Clyde valleys; it was settled by Welsh Britons driven north by the Anglo-Saxons and later by Angles escaping from the Normans. - **50 David Lloyd George**: 1863-1945, Welsh Liberal statesman, member of the Liberal Party, prime minister (1916-22); as chancellor of the exchequer (minister responsible for finances) he introduced old age pensions and an insurance scheme - **53 Merlin**: in the legends about King Arthur (see info "A British Chronology", p. 7) a man with magic powers - **55 establishment**: the group of people in society who have a lot of power and influence - **60 Stanley Baldwin**: 1867-1947, English Conservative statesman, prime minister (1923-24, 1924-29, 1932-37) - **66 second cousin twice removed**: the child of your father's cousin - **75 baron**: the lowest rank of British nobility - **79 blind man's buff** (n.): a children's game: *Blindekuh* - **85 MBE**: Member of the Order of the British Empire; a special honour given to some British people for things they have done for their country - **86 upper crust**: (inf.) the group of people who belong to the highest social class - **86 Caernarfon** /kə'nɑːvən/: (also Caernarvon) a port and resort in northwest Wales. The investiture of Prince Charles took place at Caernarvon castle in 1969. - **94 glass wall**: an unseen but powerful barrier - **95 Anglian**: here: English - **101 local authority**: people elected or paid to be the government of a particular area - **105 Powys**: a county in eastern Wales; a former kingdom of Wales - **105 Flood**: the great flood described in the Bible - **106 National Eisteddfod** /aɪs'teðvəd/: an annual festival in Wales in which competitions are held in music, drama and poetry - **111 MTV**: Music Television - **121 Social Club**: club where people meet - **125 Western Samoa**: the western part of a group of islands in the south Pacific, northeast of Fiji, which gained independence from New Zealand in 1962 - **144 Excalibur**: the magic sword of King Arthur; on his death it was thrown into a lake - **146 Cwm Pennant**: /ˌkʊm 'penant/ *cwm* = valley in Welsh; in Caernarfon, northwest Wales

Awareness

1 Make notes on what you know about Wales.

Comprehension

2 What reasons does Williams give for the defeat of the Welsh (or Britons) by the Anglo-Saxon invaders?
3 What advantages did the Welsh gain from being linked to the English?
4 What, according to the author, are the characteristics of the Anglo-Saxons and of the Welsh?
5 What, according to the author, are the characteristics of Welsh life?
6 What are the differences between the Welsh of North Wales and those of South Wales?

Analysis

7 Find examples of humour in the extract and work out how they function and what effect they are designed to achieve.
8 Characterise in your own words the impression the author gives in this extract of the Welsh and the English.
9 What is the function of the story Williams tells about his uncle Huw?

Opinion

10 Comment on the author's statement that Welsh culture "like all civilised life, [...] is threatened by Coca-Cola culture and MTV". (II. 110f.)

Projects

11 Find out about some of the most important aspects of Welsh life and culture: the Welsh language, the National Eisteddfod, Plaid Cymru (The Welsh National Party), David Lloyd George, and the Welsh poet Dylan Thomas.
12 Look at the results of the 1997 referendum in Wales. What do they tell us about Wales?

Info

Wales - Language

The easiest way of gaining entry into Welsh is probably through place names, with their recurring prefixes. *Aber-* means the point at which one river meets another or where a river runs into the sea. *Ystrad* refers to a place on the valley floor. *Llan* can be translated as 'church of', although is often incorrectly replaced by 'Saint' in English. *Tre* is the equivalent of the English 'ton', or 'town' and *Caer* of 'chester' derived from the Roman word for camp (castra). Other common prefixes are: *cwm* for valley, *din* for fort, *pen* for headland or peninsular, *tref* for farm, *pont* for bridge, and *porth* for port.

The famous *Llanfairpwllgwyngyllgogerychwyrndrobwllllantysiliogogogoch* (the Church of Mary in the hollow of the white hazel near the rapid whirlpool of the Church of Tysilio of the red cave) is strictly for tourists: the Welsh, who are tired of the joke, use '*Llanfairpwll*' or simply '*Llanfair PG*' among themselves.

The Welsh are famous for their singing, and in particular their choral singing. This hymn is often sung when Wales plays at international rugby matches, rugby being the Welsh national sport (see glossary p. 51):

ARGLWYDD, arwain trwy'r anialwch,
Fi, bererin gwael ei wedd,
Nad oes ynof nerth na bywyd,
Fel yn gorwedd yn y bedd:
Hollalluog
Ydyw'r Un a'm cwyd i'r lan!

Agor y ffynhonnau melys
Sydd yn tarddu o'r graig i maes;
Hyd yr anial maith canlyned
Afon iachawdwriaeth gras:
Rho im hynny -
Dim i mi ond dy fwynhau.

William Williams, Pantycelyn *(1717-91)*

GUIDE me, O thou great Jehovah!
Pilgrim through this barren land,
I am weak, but thou art mighty,
Hold me with thy powerful hand;
Bread of heaven,
Feed me now and evermore.

Open now the crystal fountain
Whence the healing streams do flow;
Let the fiery cloudy pillar
Lead me all my journey through:
Strong Deliverer!
Be thou still my strength and shield.

Translation Peter Williams (1723-96)

As you can see from the above the Welsh language has no connection with English.

Two thousand years ago the great Empire of Rome came with its batallions and conquered that part of Caernarvonshire in which my constituency is situated. They built walls and fortifications as the tokens of their conquest and they proscribed the use of the Cymric tongue. The other day I was glancing at the ruins of those walls. Underneath I noted the children at play, and I could hear them speaking, with undiminished force and vigour, the proscribed language of the conquered nation. Close by there was a school, where the language of the Roman conquerors was being taught, but taught as a dead language.

David Lloyd George (1863-1945) Welsh Liberal statesman, prime minister (1916-22) in Peter Hennessy, Whitehall *(London: Fontana, 1990), p. 469.*

10 | Jan Morris
"The Welsh Dragon"*

Jan Morris, who was born in 1926, is of Anglo-Welsh parentage, her mother English and her father Welsh. Her time is divided between her library-house in North Wales, her country cottage in the Black Mountains of South Wales, and travel abroad. She is an honorary D. Litt. (= Dr of Letters; Latin: *Doctor Litterarum*) of the University of Wales, an honorary Fellow (= senior teacher at a university) of University College of Aberystwyth (= town in central Wales on the coast of Cardigan Bay), and a member of the Gorsedd of Bards (= assembly or council of Welsh poets). Apart from having written six volumes of travel essays, three books on Wales, and two autobiographical works, she is a distinguished historian.

Vocabulary

3 chimera (n.): /kaɪ'mɪərə/ an imaginary creature that breathes fire, has a lion's head, a goat's body, and a snake's tail - **6 to bestride** (v.): to sit or stand on or over s.th. with one leg on each side of it - **8 coat of arms** (n.): a set of pictures or patterns painted on a shield and used as the special sign of family, town, university etc. - **9 to embellish** (v.): to make s.th. more beautiful by adding decorations - **9 host** (n.): here: large number - **10 to ennoble** (v.) here: to make s.th. seem of good quality - **12 guise** (n.): /gaɪz/ the appearance of s.th. that makes it seem different from how it really is - **14 to emblazon on** (v.): to put a name, design, picture on s.th. so that it can easily be seen - **16 rampant** (adj.): here: standing on its two back legs - **16 civic** (adj.): connected with a town or city - **17 air** (n.): appearance - **18 apotheosis** (n.): the best and most perfect example of s.th. - **18 to afford** (v.): to provide - **19 to mould** (v.): to shape - **21 diapason** (n.): /daɪə'peɪsən/ here: the largest pipes of an organ - **21 treble** (n.): higher notes; the upper half of the whole range of musical notes - **23 to prance** (v.): to walk moving your body in a confident way in order to make people notice and admire you - **23 pitch** (n.): a specially marked out area of ground on which a sport is played - **26 admonitory** (adj.): warning - **29 mnemonics** (n.): /nɪ'mɒnɪks/ s.th. such as a poem, or a sentence that you use to help you remember a rule, a name etc. - **34 vile** (adj.): very unpleasant - **37 malicious** (adj.): /mə'lɪʃəs/ showing a desire to harm s.o. - **38 fatally** (adv.): in a way that causes death - **39 carcass** (n.): the body of a dead animal - **40 serpent** (n.): snake - **41 pestilential** (adj.): extremely unpleasant and annoying - **42 crest** (n.): a raised area on the body of an animal - **43 peacock** (n.): a large male bird which has long tail feathers that it can spread out, showing their beautiful blue and green colours and patterns - **48 hillock** (n.): a little hill - **50 site** (n.): a place where s.th. important or interesting happened - **61 to disclose** (v.): to make s.th. publicly known - **66 to writhe** (v.): to twist your body from side to side violently - **73 tump** (n.): (dial.) a small rounded hill - **76 to squabble** (v.): to quarrel continuously - **78 griffin** (n.): an imaginary animal in stories that has a lion's body and an eagle's head and wings - **79 banner** (n.): flag

Explanations

18 Usk: a town in South Wales, in the county of Monmouthshire - **23 rugby football**: a type of football played with an oval ball that you can catch and carry in your hands - **25 *Croeso i Gymru***: /'krɔɪsəʊ‿iː‿'gʌmrɪ/: Welsh for "Welcome to Wales" - **30 Triads**: a Welsh form of literary composition with an arrangement of subjects or statements in groups of three - **33 Powys**: a county of east central Wales, a former kingdom of Wales - **35 *carrog***: Welsh for a small river - **40 Glamorgan**: a former county of South Wales - **47 Gwynedd** /'gwɪneð/: a county of northwest Wales, named after a former principality conquered by the English in 1282 - **48 Beddgelert** /beɪð'gelət/: a village in north Wales, in the county of Gwynneth - **53 Gwyrtheyrn (Welsh)** /'gwiːəθaɪən/ **or Vortigern (English)**: the Celtic British king who asked for the help of the Saxons under the brothers Hengist and Horsa in fighting the Picts and the Scots. They landed in Kent in about 450 AD - **60 Myrddin** /'mʌrðɪn/: the Welsh name for Merlin - **60 Merlin**: a magician who helped and supported King Arthur - **68 Saxon**: see glossary on p. 51 - **72 Dinas Emrys** /'diːnəs'emrɪs/: (Welsh) Fort of Emrys, from *din*, Welsh for fort and Emrys, a man's name

Awareness

1 What stories about mythical creatures do you know? Retell a myth you know and explain its meaning.

Comprehension

2 Think of a heading for each paragraph.

Analysis

3 Comment on the style and tone of the language used in the first paragraph. Explain why you think it was written in this way.
4 What functions does the Welsh dragon, as described in this text, have for Welsh society?
5 What do you think is the significance of the story about the Red Dragon in the third paragraph?
6 What malevolent and what benevolent characteristics do the dragons described in the text have? What do these characteristics tell us about the Welsh dragon and the Welsh people?

Project

7 Trace the history of Welsh contact with their "ancient enemy", the English.

11 R. Gerallt Jones "The Letter"

R(obert) Gerallt Jones was born in 1933 and studied at the University of Wales. He has since then been a schoolteacher, lecturer in education, principal of a teachers' training college in Jamaica, warden and headmaster of Llanovery College, Wales, Fellow (= senior teacher at a university) in Creative Writing at the University of Wales, and senior tutor at the Extra-Mural Department of the University College of Wales. He was Warden of Gregynog Hall, University of Wales. Until his death in January 1999 he was a part-time tutor at the Department of Film and Drama at the University of Aberystwyth, a town in central Wales on the coast of Cardigan Bay. He has published several volumes of poetry, short stories, literary criticism, travel writing, dramas, and an autobiography.

Vocabulary

10 pond (n.): a small area of still water - **20 to fling** (v.): to throw s.th. quickly with a lot of force - **20 indignantly** (adv.): angrily, because you feel insulted or unfairly treated - **23 junction**: place where one railway line joins another - **24 to poke around** (v.): to look for s.th. - **27 to be tucked away** (v.): to be hidden - **29 gents** (n.): gentlemen's toilets - **33 to peer** (v.): to look very carefully or hard - **44 to swagger** (v.): to walk proudly, swinging your shoulders in a way that shows too much confidence - **47 to give s.o. the once-over** (v.): (inf.) to look at s.o. or s.th. quickly to check who they are or what they are like - **48 stock-market** (n.): market where farmers sell pigs, cows, etc. - **50 off-handedly** (adv.): not giving s.o. much time or attention when you are talking to them - **51 to peep** (v.): if s.th. peeps from somewhere, it is just possible to see it - **63 diawl** (n.): (Welsh slang) devil - **77 to snuggle up** (v.): to settle into a warm comfortable position - **91 intently** (adv.): carefully - **97 to hoot with laughter** (v.): to laugh loudly because you think s.th. is funny or stupid - **120 poker** (n.): a metal stick used to move coal or wood in a fire to make it burn better - **123 dead** (adv.): here: completely - **123 to haul** (v.): to pull - **132 missus**: /mɪsɪz/ (inf.) a man's wife; Mrs - **139 to waddle** (v.): /wɒdl/ to walk with short steps, swinging from one side to another - **139 bottom**: the part of your body that you sit on - **145 nightmare** (n.): a very frightening dream - **151 water-cress** (n.): a small plant with strong tasting green leaves that grows in water - **155 barn** (n.): here: a large building - **156 to bait** (v.): to deliberately try make s.o. angry by criticising, using rude names etc.

Explanations

4 Pwllheli /pu:θ'heli/: a small town on the north-west coast of Wales on the Lleyn Peninsula in the county of Gwynedd, a Welsh-speaking area - **4 Bangor** /'bæŋgə/: a medium sized town on the northwest coast of Wales in the county of Gwynedd, a Welsh-speaking area - **5 Math**: name of a friend of the narrator - **6 Shwsbri**: the Welsh spelling of Shrewsbury, a town in the county of Shropshire in England near the border with Wales - **8 Llaniestyn** /læn'jestɪn/: a small village on the northwest coast of Wales on the Lleyn Peninsular in the county of Gwynedd, a Welsh-speaking area - **12 Felin Eithin** /'velɪn'aɪθɪn/: the name of a working flour mill, which supplied the village of Llaniestyn with bread - **15 Mam**: (dial.) Mum; mother - **20 *Hotspur***: a boys' comic - **20 Criccieth** /'krɪkjeθ/: a small town not far from Pwllheli - **79 Welshpool**: a town in Wales in the county of Montgomery near the border with England - **82 swishing**: (schoolboy sl.) smart, fashionable - **82 brekker**: (schoolboy sl.) breakfast - **83 footer**: (schoolboy sl.) football - **83 prep**: (schoolboy sl.) homework - **86 Podge**: nickname for a fat person - **86 freshie**: (schoolboy sl.) a boy in his first year of (secondary) school - **87 Welshie**: insulting name for a Welsh person - **94 the Saint**: a friend of the narrator's in his home village - **96 Pen Llyn** /pen'θli:n/: the Lleyn peninsular in the county of Gwynedd - **99 Priestley School**: an independent (= private) school - **102 bloody hell**: an expression of surprise - **102 fellers**: (inf.) fellows - **112 Cannonball Kidd**: a character in a comic - **113 Barmouth**: a seaside resort on the west coast of Wales in the county of Gwynedd - **132 Joni**: Welsh for Johnnie - **141 Mrs Jones the Post**: in Wales people's jobs are often added to their names because so many people have the same surname - ***letter* Spot**: name of a dog - ***letter* Llyn y Felin**: the Mill Lake

Awareness

1 Imagine you are twelve years old and are being sent away to go to school in Britain for a year. You have only been learning English for a year. Describe your feelings.

Comprehension

2 What does the extract tell you about the narrator of this story?

Analysis

3 Characterise the boys that the narrator meets on his journey to Shrewsbury. Pay particular attention to their use of language.
4 What effect do these boys have on the narrator?
5 In what ways is Joni's experience a "nightmare"? (l. 145)
6 Compare the letter Joni didn't write in the first paragraph with the one he did write at the end of the extract. Why didn't he write a more truthful letter?
7 Describe the life that Joni is leaving behind.

Opinion

8 Imagine you are Joni. Write a letter to your parents expressing your true feelings about being at Priestley school.
9 Comment on the behaviour of the English boys towards Joni and his reactions. Is this pattern of behaviour an inevitable part of adolescence?
10 Why do you think Joni's parents are sending him away to school? Do you agree or disagree with what they are doing?

Project

11 Find out as much as you can about the Welsh language (see info "Wales-Language" on pp. 40f. for a start).

12 | Stephen Castle
"After Devolution, Not Revolution But Evolution"

Vocabulary

4 hyperbole (n.): /haɪˈpɜːbəlɪ/ here: a number of statements which sound more important than they actually are - **5 stunning** (adj.): very surprising - **9 to spell** (v.): *here:* to mean - **24f. to tie o.s. up in knots**: to get into very great difficulties - **28 to coin** (v.): to invent a new word or phrase - **39 conundrum** (n.): a confusing and difficult problem - **41 pledge** (n.): a firm promise - **48 to scale back** (v.): to reduce (a plan or organisation) - **56 in deference to**: because of; out of respect for - **60 exempt (from)** (adj.): given special permission not to do s.th. that would normally have to be done - **74 to prompt** (v.): to make s.o. decide to do s.th. that they had been thinking of doing - **80 to dispose of** (v.): here: to have available to spend - **88 pre-requisite** (n.): (also prerequisite) s.th. s.o. must have before they can be allowed to do s.th. - **90 to tread carefully**: to be very careful about what you do in a difficult situation - **109 anomalous** (adj.): /əˈnɒmələs/ different from what you expected to find

Explanations

***Title* devolution** (n.): the act of giving power from a national government to a group or organization at a more local level (see also info "Devolution", p. 45) - **8 Welsh Office**: the government department responsible for the administration of Wales - **11 backbench**: an ordinary MP who is not one of the party leaders - **28 West Lothian**: the constituency (= area of the country represented by an MP) of Tam Dalyell from 1962-1983. Tam Dalyell is now MP for Linlithgow. (See glossary p. 51) - **31 Westminster**: here: the British government (from the district in London where parliament is situated) - **32 constituency**: area of the country represented by an MP - **46 quango**: /ˈkwæŋgəʊ/ an independent organisation started by the government but with its own legal powers (from quasi-autonomous non-governmental organisation) - **52 Boundary Commission**: the organisation responsible for deciding how big constituencies should be - **55 Treasury**: the government department that controls the money that the country collects and spends - **78 f. development agency**: an organisation responsible for encouraging firms to set up and expand in a particular area. The nine regional development agencies would cover the eight English regions and London (see map p. 29) - **80 bn**: billion (one thousand million) - **100 primaries**: elections in the US at which members of political parties in one area decide who will be their party's candidate for a particular political position - **102 proportional** (also **PR**): a system of voting in elections in which all parties are represented according to the number of votes they receive - **108 first-past-the-post**: (also first past the post) a system of voting in which only the candidate wins who gets more votes than any other candidate.

Awareness

1 Scotland will get a parliament and Wales an assembly under proposals to decentralise the British political system. What are the arguments for and against an assembly or assemblies for England?

Comprehension

2 According to the article, what changes in the British political system are likely following devolution for Scotland and Wales? List changes under the following headings: a) England; b) Scotland; c) London; d) the voting system.

Analysis

3 How does the writer justify answering the rhetorical question "But will changes in Scotland and [...] Wales really have a profound effect on England?" (ll. 16ff.) with "yes" (l. 19)?
4 Explain how the Labour Party has "tied itself up in knots over devolution" (ll. 24f.).
5 What would be the results of London having an assembly and a directly elected mayor?
6 Why are John Prescott's proposals referred to as being "evolutionary, rather than revolutionary" (ll. 83f.)?
7 Why does the writer describe the first-past-the-post system of voting used for the British parliament at Westminster as "increasingly anomolous" (l. 109)?

Opinion

8 The writer quotes two remarks which are critical of the British political system. One talks of the 'anachronistic rituals and centralising elitism of the old system' (ll. 9f.) and the other of a 'democratic deficit' (l. 89) in the English regions. Explain what you think these remarks mean and give your own ideas on possible reforms.
9 What political consequences can be drawn from Tam Dalyell's West Lothian question? Consult this term in the explanations and the glossary.
10 Write a letter to the *Independent on Sunday* giving arguments for the creation of an English parliament.

Project

11 Organise a debate on the pros and cons of devolution and on the position of England in this process.

Info

Devolution

Although the United Kingdom is composed of four nations, English, Scottish, Welsh and (Northern) Irish, it is at the moment a unitary state. All laws are passed by the parliament at Westminster. Any powers exercised by subordinate authorities are given by parliament and can be taken away by parliament. For example, an Act of Parliament established a parliament for Northern Ireland at Stormont Castle in Belfast, but in 1972 parliament suspended Stormont and imposed direct rule from London.

Taking Northern Ireland, and the proposals for Scotland and Wales as a model, devolution can be defined as:

"... the transfer to a subordinate elected body on a geographical basis, of functions at present exercised by Parliament. These functions may be either legislative, the power to make laws, or executive, the power to make decisions within an already established legal framework. [...]

Devolution involves the creation of an elected body subordinate to Parliament: it therefore seeks to preserve intact the supremacy of Parliament, a central feature of the British Constitution."

Vernon Bogdanor, *Devolution* (Oxford: Oxford University Press, 1979), p. 2.

It is therefore not the same as federalism, which, as in Germany and the United States, divides supreme power between parliament and various provincial, regional or state bodies. In federal states the powers of central and regional bodies are defined by a codified constitution. Under the British system of devolution, without a codified constitution or a supreme court, the Westminster parliament remains supreme and can at any time change the arrangements for the Scottish parliament, and Welsh and Northern Irish assemblies and even abolish them completely without having to consult anyone.

13 | "An Ould Orange Flute"

Vocabulary

Title **ould** (adj.): old; the spelling imitates the Northern Irish accent (see info "Eye Dialect", p. 35) - **2 ruction** (n.): disturbance; quarrel - **4 blade** (n.): an energetic young man - **9 deceyver** (n.): deceiver; the spelling imitates the Northern Irish accent (see info "Eye Dialect", p. 35) - **9 to take s.o. in** (v.): to make s.o. believe s.th. that is not true - **11 to forsake** (v.): to leave s.o. or s.th. - **13 townland** (n.): Irish town; area of land in and around a town - **14 to fly** (v.): (dial.) to flee; to leave somewhere quickly in order to escape from danger - **15 fixin's** (n.): (dial.) fixings; furniture, belongings - **15 to boot**: as well, in addition - **17 chapel** (n.): a small church - **17 to atone** (v.): to do s.th. to show you are very sorry for having done s.th. wrong - **17 deed** (n.): s.th. s.o. does that is very good or very bad - **20 choir** (n.): /'kwaɪə/ - **22 to shiver** (v.): to shake slightly because you are cold or frightened - **22 to sigh** (v.): to breathe in and out making a long sound, esp. when you are sad, bored, tired, etc. - **25 to jump** (v.): to make a quick sudden movement because you are surprised or frightened - **25 to start** (v.): see "to jump" - **25 splutter** (n.): here: a confused state - **27 charm** (n.): a piece of magic which involves saying special words - **30 Papish** (adj.): an insulting word describing s.th. connected with the Catholic Church - **32 to squeak** (v.): to make a very short high noise that is not loud - **34 to banish** (v.): to not allow s.o. or s.th. to stay in a particular place - **35 heresy** (n.): a belief that disagrees with the official principles of a particular religion, here of the Catholic Church - **36 stead** (n.): place - **37 to doom** (v.): to make s.o. or s.th. certain to fail, die, be destroyed, etc. - **38 heretic** (n.): s.o. who is guilty of heresy (see l. 35)

Explanations

Title **Orange**: Protestant (see info "A Northern Ireland Chronology" on p. 26 and glossary on p. 50) - **1 Tyrone**: one of the six counties of Northern Ireland, to the west of Belfast - **1 Dungannon**: town in the south of County Tyrone - **2 han'**: hand (see info "Eye Dialect", p. 35) - **5 Twelfth of July**: day on which marches and parades are held by the Protestant community in Northern Ireland to celebrate the Battle of the Boyne in Ireland in 1690 (see info "A Northern Ireland Chronology" on p. 26) - **11 Papish**: Papist; an insulting word for s.o. who supports the Catholic Church, a Catholic (see glossary p. 50) - **14 Connaught**: /'kɒnɔːt/ a county in the west of the Republic of Ireland - **18 Pater**: *paternoster*; in the Catholic Church the Lord's Prayer, esp. in Latin - **18 Ave**: (Latin: Hail Mary) Ave Maria; a prayer to the Virgin Mary used chiefly by Roman Catholics, beginning with part of Luke 1:28 - **18 beads**: the beads of the rosary, a string of beads for keeping count in prayers and devotions of the Catholic Church - **22 alas**: (arch.) an expression of sadness - **24 The Protestant Boys**: a Protestant marching song - **26 Holy Water**: water blessed by a priest and used in religious ceremonies of the Catholic Church - **28 Croppies Lie Down**: a Protestant anti-Catholic song; the croppies in the title are Catholic boys, so called because of their short (cropped) hair - **31 Kick the Pope**: a Protestant anti-Catholic song - **31 The Boyne Water**: a Protestant song celebrating the Battle of the Boyne in 1690 (see info "A Northern Ireland Chronology" on p. 26)

Awareness

1 What do you know about Northern Ireland and its inhabitants?

Comprehension

2 Write a brief summary of each stanza of the ballad in your own words.

Analysis

3 What picture of the Protestant inhabitants of Northern Ireland is created by this song? In what ways is this picture positive and in what ways negative?
4 How are the Catholic inhabitants of Northern Ireland portrayed in this song? What positive and what negative elements can you find?
5 What do you think the flute symbolises?
6 What point of view seems to be taken by the poetic narrator?

Opinion

7 What serious message(s) do you think can be found in this song?

Project

8 Using the names of the two characters in the ballad as a starting point, find out about differences, social, cultural, and historical, between the Nationalist and Unionist communities in Northern Ireland.

14 | Bernard MacLaverty "Walking the Dog"

Bernard MacLaverty was born in 1942 in Belfast. After leaving school he worked as a medical laboratory technician before taking a degree at Queen's University, Belfast in 1974. Besides the novels *Lamb* (1980), *Cal* (1983), *Grace Notes* (1997) and numerous short stories, MacLaverty has also written children's books and a screenplay. He now lives in Scotland.

Vocabulary

3 fuckin (adj.): (taboo) spelling imitates the Northern Irish accent (see info "Eye Dialect" p. 35) - **3 to beckon** (v.): to make a signal to s.o. with your hand or arm, to show you want them to come towards you - **7 to leap** (v.): to jump - **9 hound** (n.): here: an insulting word for dog - **15 to shove** /ʃʌv/ (v.): to push s.o. or s.th. in a rough or careless way - **21 upholstery** (n.): material used to cover chairs, car seats, etc. - **23 to pant** (v.): to breath quickly using short noisy breaths because you have been running or because it is very hot - **24 nape** (n.): the back of your neck - **28 right-oh**: here: a signal to the driver to move off - **32 aye**: (dial.) yes - **32 mebby** (adv.): maybe; imitation of Northern Irish accent. See info box on "Eye Dialect" on p. 35. - **53 to shrug** (v.): to raise and then lower your shoulders in order to show you do not know s.th. or do not care about s.th. - **54 ridge** (n.): a long narrow raised part of a surface - **55 drive shaft** (n.): a part of a vehicle that takes power from the gearbox to the wheels - **66 to wag** (v.): here: to move repeatedly from one side to the other - **76 staggering** (adj.): so great as to be almost unbelievable - **79 butt** (n.): the thick end of the handle (of a gun) - **80 cheek** (n.): disrespectful or rude behaviour - **84 to groan** (v.): to make a long deep sound because you are in pain - **88 to growl** (v.): (of an animal) to make a long deep angry sound - **89 blow** (n.): a hard hit with the hand, a tool, or a weapon - **93 to come to it in one**: to come to the point quickly - **101 crap** (n.): (taboo) s.th. s.o. says that you think is completely wrong or untrue - **103 wanker** (n.): (taboo) s.o. you think is stupid or unpleasant - **117 to steel o.s.** (v.): to prepare o.s. for s.th. that you know will be unpleasant - **131 to vouch for s.o.** (v.): to say that you believe that what s.o. has said is true - **133 muzzle** (n.): the end of the barrel of a gun - **135 vertebrae** (n.): the small bones down the centre of your back - **152 dud** (n.): s.th. that is useless or worthless (here because John Shields does not seem to be a Catholic) - **157 to catch o.s. on** (v.): (dial.) not to be stupid - **159 naw**: (dial.) no - **165 pimple** (n.): small raised points for blind people to indicate where the pavement ends - **167 to save s.o.'s bacon**: (inf.) to save s.o. from danger - **180 persuasion** (n.): here: strongly held belief or opinion - **185 to rack** (v.): here: to pull

Explanations

42 IRA: Irish Republican Army (see glossary p. 50) - **51 John Shields**: the name does not give a clear indication of the person's religion, Catholic or Protestant. - **78 bastard**: (taboo) a word for s.o. esp. s.o. you think is unpleasant - **110 Lisburn Road**: a main road leading out of Belfast in a southwesterly direction through mainly Protestant areas - **112 the Falls**: an area around the Falls Road in the southwest of Belfast, a mainly Catholic area - **112 Republican**: supporting the idea of a united Ireland, not wanting Northern Ireland to be part of the United Kingdom (see glossary p. 51) - **112 safe house**: a house where s.o. can hide when their enemies are looking for them - **126 aitch, haitch**: the myth is that Protestants pronounce the letter h "aitch" and that Catholics pronounce it "haitch" - **128 smart Alec**: (inf.) s.o. who always says clever things or always has the right answer in a way that is annoying - **138 Mastermind**: a television programme in which people's general knowledge is tested - **139 Provos**: the Provisional IRA (see glossary p. 50) - **145 Gas Board**: the nationalised company which used to be responsible for the distribution and sale of gas. It has now been privatised and is called BG. - **146 meter man**: the man from the gas company who comes to your house to look at the gas meter to see how much gas you have used and tell you how much you must pay - **147 E.O.**: Executive Officer; a high grade of employee in the Gas Board - **150 Fenian**: originally the name for a member of the Irish Republican Brotherhood, a 19th century revolutionary nationalist organisation among the Irish in the US and Ireland, now mainly in Northern Ireland an offensive name, used by Protestants, for Catholics - **167 Hail Mary**: a prayer to the Virgin Mary used chiefly by Roman Catholics, beginning with part of Luke 1:28; also called Ave Maria

Awareness

1 What comes to mind when you think of the expression "walking the dog"?
2 Imagine you are out walking your dog. Think of incidents that might occur which would prevent you getting home on time.

Comprehension

3 What indicates that John Shields is a Protestant?

Analysis

4 Much of the extract is in the form of dialogue. Characterise the language used by the driver and his accomplice on the one hand and John Shields on the other. Use the info "Eye Dialect" on p. 35.
5 What does John Shields learn about the two gunmen during the journey?
6 We perceive the car journey from John Shield's point of view. Explain how the author creates a vivid description of the journey in spite of the fact that John Shields cannot clearly see what is happening.
7 How does the writer create tension in this extract?

Opinion

8 What might be the motives for the two men in the car wanting to kill Catholics?
9 To what extent, if any, does this story seem to be for or against the Protestants or Catholics in Northern Ireland?

Project

10 Write an imaginary letter in which John Shields describes his feelings about what happened to him.

General Projects

National and regional identity is not just a question of politics. How closely we feel linked to another group of people is a result of many factors: language, religion, clothing and costume, food and drink, appearance, customs and habits, a common history, sports, music and dance, and shared myths and symbols.

A study of any of these topics with reference to the nations and regions of the British Isles would make a fascinating and rewarding project. Some suggestions for possible projects are:

1 **Languages and dialects of the British Isles:** Scotland: Gaelic, Lowlands Scots or Lallands and Scottish English; Wales: Welsh, Welsh English; Northern Ireland: Irish Gaelic or Erse, Ulster English; England: some English dialects and accents - Cockney, Northern English vs Southern English, Geordie (Newcastle dialect), Scouse or Liverpudlian (Liverpool dialect).

2 **Sports:** origins of Rugby League and Rugby Union; the significance of rugby for Wales and Northern England; Gaelic football in Northern Ireland; the Highland Games and Scottish sports; cricket in England.

3 **Religion:** the significance of religion and sectarianism in Northern Ireland and Scotland; England as a Protestant state; the significance of the chapel in Wales.

4 **Clothing and costume:** Scotland: the kilt; folk costumes in England and Wales.

5 **Music and dance:** Scotland: the bagpipes and Scottish folk dances; England: folk dances (Morris dancing); Wales: the choirs and singing.

6 **Food and drink:** England: the pub and its role in social life; English ale; English tea; English dishes: e.g. cauliflower cheese, the English breakfast, fish and chips; Scotland: whisky, porridge, haggis (see below), Wales: Welsh rarebit.

To start you off, here is a classic Scottish dish traditionally eaten on Burns night, 25 January and St Andrew's Day, 30 November, carried high on a silver tray by a Highlander in full Highland dress, preceded by a piper playing a national tune.

Haggis with tatties (potatoes) and neeps (turnips)

1 stomach bag of a sheep
liver, lungs, and heart of a sheep
1 breakfast cup of oatmeal
2 onions
8 oz (ounces) shredded mutton suet
salt, black pepper

Clean stomach bag thoroughly and leave overnight in cold water to which salt has been added. Turn rough side out. Put heart, lungs, and liver in a pan. Bring to the boil and simmer for 1/2 hours. Toast the oatmeal on a tray in the oven or under the grill. Chop the heart, lungs and liver. Mix all the ingredients together with the suet, adding salt and pepper. Keep the mixture moist, using the liquid in which the liver was boiled. Fill the stomach bag a little over half full, as the mixture needs to swell. Sew securely and put in a large pot of hot water. As soon as the mixture begins to swell, prick with a needle to prevent the bag from bursting. Boil for 3 hours.
Serve with mashed potatoes and mashed turnip. Serves 6-8.

Or, buy a haggis from a good butcher in northern England or Scotland!

Resources for Projects

The first place to look for project materials is your school library and resource centre. Information is also often available at town or county libraries. Never write away for information you can get locally or from reference books. These might include:

- dictionaries of various kinds,
- encyclopaedias both in your own language and in English
- books about Britain
- the internet

When you *have* to contact an organisation for information, research your subject thoroughly *first*, then ensure that your query is factual and something which can be answered reasonably quickly. Remember it is no one's job to do your work for you. You might want to contact institutions concerned with English-speaking countries, such as the British Council.

Glossary

Accent: this refers to differences in pronunciation, usually but not always, those that indicate a person's regional or social origins or identity. For example, certain features of accent differentiate British from American speakers: car BE /kɑː/ vs AE /kɑːr/, path BE /pɑːθ/ vs AE /pæθ/, or Southern English from Northern English speakers: but /bʌt/ vs /bʊt/, or Cockney from RP (Received Pronunciation) nothing /nʌfɪn/ vs /nʌθɪŋ/. (See also Received Pronunciation)

Britons: this term can refer to a) the pre-Celtic inhabitants of Britain; b) the Celtic inhabitants of Britain; and c) the modern inhabitants of Britain. The last use of the word is very rare in spoken English and is confined to formal literary use. To quote H.W. Fowler: "no Englishman, and perhaps no Scot even, calls himself a Briton without a sneaking sense of the ludicrous."[1]

[1] *Modern English Usage* (1926), p. 139.

Catholic: in the 1991 census (= counting people and their opinion), 38.4 per cent of the population of Northern Ireland considered themselves to be Roman Catholics. This part of the population is mainly Irish by culture and history, and the majority of them favour a united Ireland. In the 1997 general election the two parties which supported moves towards a united Ireland, and received votes from the Catholic part of the population, Sinn Fein and the Social Democratic and Labour Party (SDLP), gained 40.2% of the total vote.

Celts: they were not the original inhabitants of Britain. When the Celts started to arrive in Britain from central Europe in about 700 BC, they had to fight native Britons who had been there for over 3000 years. The Celts brought with them their language, which is still spoken in Wales, Scotland, and Ireland, their skills in arts and crafts, and their religion, with its priests, the druids.

Danes: in English history the term Danes is usually synonymous with Vikings and often includes the other Scandinavians, Swedes and Norwegians. The first Danish attacks on England took place at the end of the eighth century, the first recorded raids being in 789-802. In 865 and 892 the Danes invaded in force and the armies settled permanently throughout eastern and northern England. They also left a permanent mark on the English language. Further invasions took place at the end of the tenth century, when England became part of a Viking empire under Canute, which included Denmark, Norway and parts of western France.

Dialect: this refers to a language variety in which accent, grammar and vocabulary indicate a person's regional or social origins or identity. A regional dialect gives us information about the speaker's geographical origin; a social dialect gives us information about the speaker's class, social status, and educational background. For example, the use of 'as' in 'He's a man as likes his beer' indicates that the speaker comes from the Midlands region of England. The use of 'of' instead of 'to' in 'It's a quarter of four' indicates that the speaker is American rather than British.
Dialect is often used in a negative way, as when someone refers to the speech of an area as "just a dialect". In fact we all speak a dialect of a language, even those who speak the standard variety or dialect. In the case of English, Standard English is simply the dialect of English that has been adopted as the norm for educated use. In the case of German, the standard dialect is called *Hochdeutsch*. (See also slang).

Good Friday Agreement, 1998: The Irish government gives up its claim to Northern Ireland; an assembly of 108 members will be set up; an executive with responsibilities for education, health, economic development, social services, finance, environment and agriculture, will only be able to take decisions with agreement from both the Nationalist and Unionist sides in the assembly; a body representing both Northern Ireland and the Irish Republic will be created; a human rights commission and an equality commission will be set up; all prisoners linked to an organisation involved in the conflict will be released within two years; the use of Gaelic is to be encouraged where there is a demand for it; referendums will be held if it seems likely that a majority of those voting would prefer Northern Ireland to leave the United Kingdom and to form part of a united Ireland.

IRA: Irish Republican Army; the IRA was founded in 1919 as a guerilla force to fight for a united Ireland. When civil unrest broke out in Northern Ireland in 1969 the IRA did not mobilise immediately. When it did the movement split into two: the Provisional IRA (also called Provos and Provisionals) together with its political wing Sinn Fein and the Official IRA. The Official IRA preferred mainly political action to secure a united Ireland whereas the Provisional IRA started a terrorist campaign – which it called a military campaign – against British rule in Northern Ireland. Over 3,300 people have died in the so-called Troubles, over 2,000 killed by the Provisionals. They have also killed about 50 in attacks on the British mainland and in continental Europe. The movement is financed by criminal activities, and fund-raising in Ireland, Britain and the United States.

Normans: the Normans, as the name suggests 'Northmen' were descendants of Vikings who had settled in Normandy in the ninth century. By the time of the Norman conquest in 1066, however, the Normans no longer spoke Danish but Norman French.

Provos: see IRA.

Protestant: according to the1991 census (= counting people and their opinion), 50.6 per cent of the population of Northern Ireland regard themselves as Protestant. Most of them are descendants of Scots and English settlers, are British by culture and tradition, and are committed to the Union between Northern Ireland and the rest of the United Kingdom. Politically their votes are cast for the parties that call themselves "Unionist", and in the 1997 general election these parties (Ulster Unionist, Democratic Unionist, United Kingdom Unionist, Progressive Unionist) received 49.3% of the total vote.

Received Pronunciation or RP: this is an accent of English which is not restricted to any region and has high social prestige in England. At one time it was the only accent used on BBC radio and television and is also known as BBC English. Nowadays a wide range of accents can be heard on BBC and only newsreaders use RP exclusively. Like all accents RP is subject to change and variation and the RP of the 1990s is very different from the RP of the 1930s. It has been estimated that only about 5% of British English speakers use RP. Many more use what is called modified RP: RP with a slight regional or social influence.

Republican: this term is usually used to refer militant supporters of a united Ireland and to Sinn Fein, the Irish political party with links to the IRA (Irish Republican Army).

Romans: the Romans invaded Britain twice. The first time under Julius Caesar was in 55 BC. But Caesar withdrew the next year and it was not until AD 43 that the Romans returned. When the Romans left in 410 AD it was because of increasing attacks on the Empire from across the Rhine and the Danube.

Rugby: the Welsh are traditionally mad about rugby. Even though the game was invented in England, at Rugby School (in the middle of the 19th century), the Welsh regularly beat the English at it. Rugby matches enable the Welsh to combine their love of the sport and of singing. The Welsh play rugby union, a form of rugby played by teams of fifteen, unlike rugby league, which has teams of thirteen.
Rugby is played with an oval ball which may be kicked, carried and passed by hand. Points are scored by placing the ball on the ground behind the opponents' goal line (thereby scoring a 'try') or by kicking it between the two posts and over the crossbar of the opponents' goal.

Saxon: the term used by the Welsh, who are descended from the original Celtic inhabitants of Britain, to describe the Anglo-Saxon invaders of Celtic Britain. The Anglo-Saxon invasion of Britain by the Angles, Saxons and Jutes from northern Europe started in about 440 AD, after the Romans had left Britain.

Slang: this has nothing to do with either accent or dialect. It is informal, nonstandard vocabulary which can occur in all varieties and dialects. It can take the form of dialect words, invented words, abbreviations, metaphor, metonymy and word play, such as rhyming slang, and is usually used either as a mark of social identity – to indicate that the speaker belongs to a special group, such as doctors, students, sailors – or to show that the speech situation is particularly informal. In practice it is often difficult to draw a dividing line between words which are informal and colloquial and those which are slang. The verb 'to booze' for 'to drink alcohol, especially too much' is considered informal in some English dictionaries and slang in others. Some words like 'mob' have entered the standard language from slang.

West Lothian Question: this problem was pointed out by the Scottish MP, Tam Dalyell, an opponent of devolution. As a result of devolution Wales and Scotland will have their own parliament or assembly, but will continue to send MPs to the United Kingdom parliament at Westminster. As a result of devolution, the main task of the UK parliament will be to govern England. This means that English MPs will have little say about what goes on in Wales and Scotland but Welsh and Scottish MPs (including Tam Dalyell, who was the MP for West Lothian from 1962-83, and is now MP for Linlithgow) will have a say in what goes on in England. It has been pointed out that this situation has been in operation in the case of Northern Ireland since 1922, which until the abolition of the Northern Ireland parliament at Stormont also sent and still sends MPs to Westminster. These MPs from Northern Ireland voted on matters connected with England, whereas the UK parliament had very little influence on what happened in Northern Ireland.

William the Conqueror: also William I and William of Normandy. He claimed to have been promised the English crown by Edward the Confessor. On Edward's death both he and Harold II claimed the English throne. He invaded England in 1066 and defeated Harold at the Battle of Hastings. After the conquest he introduced Norman institutions and customs, including feudalism. Normandy was a province of northern France that had been settled by the Vikings or Northmen (from whom the name is derived) in the tenth century.

Acknowledgements

The material reproduced in this book has been taken from the following sources:

Photographs and Illustrations

Action Press, Hamburg: page 16 (middle) -
Archiv für Kunst und Geschichte, Berlin: page 13 (top), 16 (left) -
"The Bayeux Tapestry - 11th Century" by special permission of the City of Bayeux: page 2 -
Blackwell Publishers, Oxford: page 29 (left) -
British Tourist Authority, London: page 6 (left), 7 (middle) (top), 11 (bottom) -
British Tourist Authority, Frankfurt: page 12, 13 (bottom), 17 (top), 19, 26 -
Corel Stock Photo Library: Cover (bottom right), page 13 (bottom) -
Eva Gleifenstein, München: page 28, 49 -
Guardian Newspapers Ltd., London: page 5 (top) (bottom) -
The Image Bank Bildagentur, München: Cover (background) -
Impact Photos, London: page 9 (bottom), 23 -
keine Angaben über ©-Holder: page 29 (right)
Ham Kahn, Argentina: page 11 (top) -
Laenderpress GmbH, Mainz: page 6 (right) -
North News and Pictures, Newcastle upon Tyne: page 5 (middle) -
Private Eye, London: page 24, 25 -
PWE Verlag GmbH, Hamburg: page 7 (bottom), 10 -
Sportimage Fotoagentur GmbH, Hamburg: page 17 (bottom) -
Superbild Bildarchiv Erich Bach, Grünwald: Cover (flags)
Time & Life Syndication, New York: page 1 (top) -
The Sunday Times, London: page 1 (bottom) -
Times Newspapers Limited, 10 Jan 1999: page 9 (top) -
Wales Tourist Board, Cardiff: page 41 -
John Walmsley, Guildford: page 16 (right), 18, 20 -
Zefa Zentrale Farbbild Agentur GmbH, Düsseldorf: page 4, 8

Texts

BBC Worldwide, London: page 15 -
The Blackstaff Press Ltd., Belfast: page 23 -
The Daily Mail, London: page 11 -
Guardian Newspapers Ltd., London: page 5 -
Hodder & Stoughton Ltd., London: page 2 -
Independent Newspapers Ltd., London: page 21 -
John McIntyre: page 8 -
Oxford University Press, Oxford: page 18 -
Penguin Books Ltd., London: page 17, 24 -
Billy Wolfe, Kaimend, Scotland: page 10 -